Desiree Ayres manifests a ⁚ ner of gracious womanline⁚ dynamic quality of leadersl some, and spiritually potent communicator—with all these qualities backed up by a purity of heart, strength of character, and a Christ-like genuineness. I am honored to be called "Pastor" by both her and her husband, Mel.

—JACK W. HAYFORD
PRESIDENT, INTERNATIONAL FOURSQUARE CHURCH
CHANCELLOR, THE KING'S COLLEGE AND SEMINARY
LOS ANGELES, CALIFORNIA

Having known Desiree Ayres and her ministry and testimony that she has shared to countless thousands over the years, I have seen firsthand the change in people's lives. I believe this book can have the same lasting impact in your life, especially in the area of anorexia, bulimia, and compulsive eating. I have seen many challenges over my lifetime and ministry, and being in the healing ministry, this book can play a major role in one's healing, especially in eating disorders.

—ORAL ROBERTS

For those who have a hunger for God, you will find that this book will be a real blessing. Follow the guidelines, precepts, and examples that are presented here and it will lead you to a life of victory and fulfillment. It shows you that God's Word is the answer to your hunger and thirst. You will find out how to be free from any addiction such as drugs, alcohol, eating disorders, unforgiveness, or anything that keeps you in bondage. We highly recommend this book.

—DRS. FRED AND BETTY PRICE

In the many years I have known Desiree Ayres I have always been impressed by her sincere love for God and true desire to help people. Desiree is living proof of how God's Word will make a way, even when we have no hope in the natural. God has done amazing things in Desiree's life, and the truth of the Word as shared in this book can, without doubt, bring about the same victory and freedom in your life as it has in hers.

—Pastor Wendy Treat
Christian Faith Center
Seattle, Washington

GOD
HUNGER

GOD
HUNGER

Jackie,
You are Beautiful!
Matthew 4:4:

Desiree Ayres

Desiree Ayres

CREATION HOUSE
A STRANG COMPANY

GOD HUNGER by Desiree Ayres
Published by Creation House
A Strang Company
600 Rinehart Road
Lake Mary, Florida 32746
www.creationhouse.com

Unless otherwise noted, all Scripture quotations are from the New
King James Version of the Bible. Copyright © 1979, 1980, 1982 by
Thomas Nelson, Inc., publishers. Used by permission.

Scripture quotations marked AMP are from the Amplified Bible. Old
Testament copyright © 1965, 1987 by the Zondervan Corporation. The
Amplified New Testament copyright © 1954, 1958, 1987 by the Lock-
man Foundation. Used by permission.

Scripture quotations marked NIV are from the Holy Bible, New International Version. Copyright © 1973, 1978, 1984, International Bible
Society. Used by permission.

Scripture quotations marked THE MESSAGE are from *The Message: The
Bible in Contemporary English*, copyright © 1993, 1994, 1995, 1996,
2000, 2001, 2002. Used by permission of NavPress Publishing Group.

Cover design by Karen Grindley

Library of Congress Control Number: 2005930412
International Standard Book Number: 1-59185-901-8

First Edition

05 06 07 08 09— 987654321
Printed in the United States of America

I DEDICATE THIS BOOK:

To my awesome, powerful man of God: my husband, my mentor, my best friend, Mel Ayres. How can I thank you enough for speaking the Word of God over me and helping me live and not die? Thank you for walking in love, truth, boldness, and strength. You are the greatest example of the love of God I have ever seen.

To the wonderful teachers of faith: Kenneth Haggin, Kenneth and Gloria Copeland, Drs. Fred and Betty Price, Dr. Oral Roberts, and others who in the midst of religious persecution continued to boldly speak the Word of God and see the multitudes set free. Thank you for not quitting and being bold for Jesus.

To every person who has ever battled an addiction: I know your hurt, I know your pain, and I know your embarrassment and frustration. I also know the One who can set you 100 percent free. Follow me through these pages as I show you what He showed me. God set me free and is using me to set others free. He will also set you free and use you to set others free. Glory to God!

To my Lord and Savior Jesus Christ, thank You for showing me the way, and healing me! I love You!

Acknowledgments

I HAVE BEEN WORKING on this book for about ten years and am thrilled to finally complete this work that I believe will touch many lives. I could not have completed it without the help of many people. A heartfelt thank you to:

- ❤ My husband, Mel Ayres, who encouraged me to write this book to help others achieve the victory I experienced through Christ.

- ❤ My awesome assistants: Elise Jones, Gladys Dodd, and Molly Rodriguez.

- ❤ My awesome editors: Renee DeLoriea, Mary Busha, and Christine Hess.

- ❤ Ginny Maxwell, project manager at Creation House.

- ❤ My mom and dad, Dori and Hubie Kerns, who have always believed in me and encouraged me to do things that I thought I could not, including writing a book.

☙ Harry and Cheryl Salem for all of your wisdom and insight you have given to me, answering my numerous questions on writing my first book. Your friendship has been an inspiration to me.

☙ All the wonderful people who went through my "God Hunger Support Group" and were set free by Jesus!

☙ And finally to all those who heard my testimony and will continue to hear it and know that God is not a respecter of persons; He will set them free as well!

CONTENTS

PREFACE

Thomas Costain's history, *The Three Edwards*, described the life of Raynald III, a fourteenth-century duke in what is now Belgium.[1] Grossly overweight, Raynald was commonly called by his Latin nickname, Crassus, which means *fat*. After a violent quarrel, Raynald's younger brother, Edward, led a successful revolt against him. Edward captured Raynald but did not kill him. Instead, he built a room around Raynald in the Nieuwkerek castle and promised him that he could regain his title and property as soon as he was able to leave the room. This would not have been difficult for most people since the room had several windows and a door of near-normal size, and none was locked or barred. The problem was Raynald's size. To regain his freedom, he needed to lose weight. But Edward knew his older brother, and each day he sent a variety of delicious foods. Instead of dieting his way out of prison, Raynald grew fatter. When Duke Edward was accused of cruelty, he had a real answer: *My brother is not a prisoner. He may leave when he wills.* Raynald stayed in that room for ten years and wasn't released until after Edward died in battle. By then his health was so ruined that he died within a year...a prisoner of his own appetite.

Could it be that you see yourself in this story? Have you been a prisoner of your own appetite? If so, here are the reasons and strategies for being set free from that prison of unhealthy living now and forevermore.

FOREWORD

W HEN DESIREE ASKED me to write the fore-
word for *God Hunger* I began to pray and seek
the Lord's direction…and I read the manu-
script. *God Hunger* can help you change your perspectives,
encourage you to continue on until your breakthrough is
manifested in your life. It is full of insights, revelations, and
intertwined in a wonderful healing testimony of a life now
filled with Jesus. It certainly didn't start that way, and that is
the most enlightening journey inside these pages.

Desiree Ayres is a friend. She is a real friend that sticks
closer than a brother (or a sister)! She and Mel were there for
Harry and me as our family went through the horrible trag-
edy of our little six-year-old daughter being stricken with
a brain tumor. After eleven months she crossed over and
was birthed into eternity. They never left us, never forsook
us. Truer friends we will never find. Their lives and their
friendship has shown us a deep measure of Christ. They are
the real deal, no faking it. There are no masks covering who
they really are.

It is in Desiree's realness and stick-to-it-tive-ness that her life is unfolded before your eyes as you read *God Hunger*. In these last days God is raising up men and women whose lives have exemplified the "fire tested" strength of going through and not giving up. We can not attain the higher levels of spiritual living while still on this earth without the very "fire" of God's presence in our everyday lives.

Desiree tells of her struggles with her self-image, eating disorders, and her true search for God. You might be shocked when you read of her dabbling in the occult, but read on; don't quit. You may laugh, cry, and even have to stop reading every so often as your heart is so touched and maybe even pricked with self awareness. But mostly, I believe that you will identify within your own life some deep and unresolved struggles that God longs for you to uncover and allow Him to heal and restore.

Don't be afraid to approach this book of overcoming and becoming all that God has called us to be. Don't put off dealing with the inner turmoil and hidden hurts that try to hide behind the masks of perfection and performance that we have so easily been trained to wear.

Let Desiree, through the power of the Holy Spirit, guide you through her own life's overcoming trials to the ultimate victory within each and every one of us. I have said for years, "What we don't overcome will ultimately overcome us." Within these pages lies the heart of a true woman after God's own heart. She may help you find your way, too. God longs for you to be most hungry for Him, for His presence, His touch than anything else this world has to offer. He longs to fill you with His divine presence and in that very act fill the voids of your life you have spent your entire existence trying to fill. Only a true hunger for eternity will allow who you were created to be to begin to blossom and bloom into the Life, Truth, and the Way in which you are searching.

We are made triune; spirit, soul, and body. We cannot reconcile one or two of these realms of our true being and not finish the course. All three dimensions of our presence complete the whole of our being. We are made in the image of God, triune, complete, and finished. The picture of your life is finished already inside of God. He has divided it up into pieces and has handed you the box with the instructions to put your life back together again.

I believe that *God Hunger* can help you find your way to total health and balance in every area of your life.

—CHERYL (PREWITT) SALEM
MISS AMERICA, 1980

INTRODUCTION

W E ARE NOW living in a day when what we look like is such a big deal that people are becoming obsessed with it.

This is a time in which some people would rather die than be fat.

This is a big problem. (Don't worry though, because there is help from our Big God.)

The diet and diet-related industry is a $50 billion a year enterprise. People are spending billions of dollars on diet, exercise, health, nutrition, and the new big one—plastic surgery.

Some people are eating their chocolate malts, cookies, and pastas, and simply making an appointment for liposuction. Liposuction is not the answer, however!

I know the answer! I can help you! I know this to be true firsthand because I was set free myself and have seen hundreds of other people set free, too.

I believe God will use this book to set you free from every addiction to which you are in bondage.

First, I will expose the problem by sharing some statistics with you. Then, we will turn our attention to the heart of the book: the solution.

If you are suffering from any type of eating disorder, or other addiction of any sort, you can be set free. You can admit it and quit it. All things are possible with our Big God. He will help you. He helped me and I am certain that He will help you, too, if you let Him.

> Eating disorders affect five- to ten million American adolescent girls and women and approximately one million American boys and men. Worldwide, approximately seventy million individuals struggle with this disorder. In an individual's lifetime, approximately fifty thousand people will die because of this terrifying disease. Eating disorders know no race, age, class, or gender. Eating disorders have been present in children as young as three years old and in adults as old as ninety.[1]

> The most common behavior that will lead to an eating disorder is dieting.[2]

> It is estimated that currently 11 percent of high school students have been diagnosed with an eating disorder.[3]

> Also, 81 percent of ten-year-olds are afraid of being fat, while 51 percent of nine- and ten-year-old girls feel better about themselves if they are on a diet.[4]

> The mortality rate for anorexia is higher than for any other psychological disorder. In fact, it's the number one cause of death among young women.[5]

Up to 19 percent of college-age women in America are bulimic.[6]

According to a recent study, over half the females between the ages of eighteen and twenty-five would prefer to be run over by a truck than be fat, and two-thirds surveyed would rather be mean or stupid.[7]

Forty-two percent of first- through third-grade girls want to be thinner.[8]

It has been shown that 80 percent of American women are disatisfied with their appearance.[9]

The three most talked-about eating disorders are anorexia nervosa (self-starvation), bulimia nervosa (binge-purge), and binge eating disorder (binging—also known as compulsive eating).[10]

Two-thirds of adults in the United States are over-weight, and 30.5 percent are obese, according to data from the 1999–2000 National Health and Nutrition Examination Survey. Approximately 300,000 adult deaths in the United States each year are attributable to unhealthy dietary habits and physical inactivity.[11]

Americans' extra weight cost the nation as much as $93 billion in annual medical bills and the government pays about half of that amount. [12]

As you can see, you are not alone in this battle. Many people are suffering from addictions. Many people are becoming unhealthier and are losing the fight. Others are becoming healthy and winning the fight. Please allow me to help you win this battle, simply by sharing with you what God has told and showed me on winning the battle. I have been set free for over twenty years and am helping others to be set free, too.

Please allow me to start by praying for you before you proceed to the solution portion of the book:

> *Dear Father God, I thank You for the person reading this book right now, and I thank You for the love that you have for this person. I thank You that he/she is not alone in this battle, for You have said, "I will fight for you and with you, I desire victory for you, I desire freedom for you! I delight to show up and reveal Myself in your life: Give Me the Glory, and you shall reap the benefit!"[13]*
>
> *Father, I thank You for great encouragement for Your child, that You would touch this person through the revelation of Your Word that has set me free! I pray hope, freedom, and victory in every area of their life! I thank You for healing every hurt, pain, and discouragement. I pray for a merry heart as he/she reads this book. I pray for dreams and visions, clarity, and every good and perfect gift coming from You, Father God, as You bless Your child. In Jesus' name I pray.*

1

HUNGRY FOR GOD

I HAVE GOOD NEWS for you. If you are suffering from any type of eating disorder, you can be 100 percent healed! I can tell you that with boldness and confidence because I have been completely healed of anorexia, bulimia, and compulsive eating.

Acts 10:34 says, "God shows no partiality and is not a respecter of persons" (AMP). That means that the same God who healed me can heal you, too.

I believe my testimony will encourage you, bring you hope and freedom, and inspire you to share your victory over eating disorders with others.

Over twenty years ago, I was in a life-and-death battle with anorexia and bulimia. At that time, following several years of abuse of food that had started destroying me on the inside, signs of the disease were showing outwardly as well. My hair was falling out and my nails were paper-thin. I needed help desperately, but I didn't know how to get it, and I certainly didn't want anyone to know the trouble I was in.

Unaware of names for my unhealthy eating habits and

exercise routines, which were sometimes planned and sometimes simply out of control, I'd go days without eating any food, starving my body. I learned that this behavior is called anorexia. Other times when I felt starved, I would eat huge amounts of food at one sitting. Then I'd feel terrible and guilty, and I'd throw it all up or take excessive amounts of laxatives and diuretics to rid my body of the excess. This is called bulimia.

My exercise routine was also obsessive. Daily I ran several miles while training for marathons, taught a couple of aerobic classes, and then would do a two-mile ocean swim. I'd follow all that with several games of volleyball.

The time came, however, when I underwent a six-month crash course from God Himself, which resulted in total victory from my eating disorders, a victory I have maintained for over twenty years. The eye-opening truth He shared with me is what I want to share with you in this book. Please enjoy and be encouraged as you journey with me on a life-changing course of events that led to my freedom and one that can lead to your freedom, too.

HUNGRY FOR GOD

Studies show that people with eating disorders can suffer from low self-esteem. The question of why I had low self-esteem was not easily answered. One thing I did know for sure, however, was that my mind was obsessed with my weight. I stood on my bathroom scale several times a day. I either ate nothing at all or I ate uncontrollably. At times it seemed I could not fill this bottomless pit. What I didn't realize was that I was starving for God. I was suffering from the number-one spiritual disease in America: God hunger! I believe we are all born with this "hunger for

God" although many of us are not aware of it. We are spirit, soul, and body, and every ounce of us cries out to be close to God, our Creator.

As a young child, I went to a Christian Science church. Additionally, since my parents had always encouraged me to be open-minded, I studied New Age religions and attended a variety of churches with friends. By the time I was fifteen, I was attending regular meetings at a small church rented by a New Age group and was being raised up and groomed to be a psychic. I was hungry for tangible spiritual experiences and for the power of God. I wanted to know Him, walk with Him, talk with Him, and do great things for Him. I was naïve in the spirit realm, however, and had no idea that, in reality, I was on the verge of losing my life while trying to walk in the supernatural.

When I was sixteen, I moved from California to Florida with my girlfriend to a waterfront cottage my grandmother owned. This seemed like an exciting adventure and an escape from the emotionally draining divorce my parents were going through. There, I became involved with another group of psychics who met weekly.

One evening as I was relaxing on my bed, I suddenly found myself on the ceiling even though my body was still on the bed. Fearful, somehow I got back down into my body. Then I immediately ran and told my brother, who was staying with us at the time and seemed to know a few things about the spirit realm. Soon after, he gave me a book on astral-projection, which is about having out-of-body experiences. The book contained all kinds of testimonies of people leaving their bodies. My brother encouraged me to try to see some of the guru-masters for more information, or for fun to go visit Mom in California. *Great*, I thought, *I can go see Mom without paying airfare!*

As I continued the practice of astral-projection, I would always end up in outer space. The last time I chose to astral-project, what I saw there would make the worst horror flick seem like a cartoon. Snake-like creatures, serpents the size of twenty-story buildings, and hideous, horrid things were trying to kill me! I focused in on "the white light," like my New Age teacher taught, but nothing happened. Over and over, I confessed, "God is love," a concept I had learned in my Christian Science teachings. Still nothing happened. In my desperation the only thing that was clear was that I was powerless to do anything!

I cried out to God, and what seemed like hours later, somehow by His mercy, I ended up back in my body, terror-stricken—and determined that I would have nothing more to do with the supernatural until I was more spiritually advanced. Because of the horror I experienced, however, I had no desire to advance.

From that point on, I stayed as far away as possible from anything that had to do with God. I decided I wanted to be a normal teenager. And besides, with my psychic training, I was tired of knowing what my friends were thinking all the time. I pushed away every form of spirituality I knew or came across.

I returned to the West Coast and during my first year of college I lived a play-filled life at San Diego State University. However, after having my heart broken by my first love, I decided to get away from California and go to my sister's Christian Science college in Illinois. My sister, Sheree, prayed for me over the years, but when I arrived at her college she saw that she had to double-up on her prayer time because I was nothing but rebellious trouble. I found other girls like me and we hitchhiked to the Ozarks, and swam in the nude while our sorority sisters were on their knees praying for us. I embarrassed and humiliated my sister with my continual wild, self-centered actions. She tried to encourage me to go to church, but to me the services there seemed powerless and boring.

OUT OF CONTROL

I was starving spiritually and began to eat to fill the emptiness. The void was so great, however, there was not enough food in all of Illinois to fill it. By my second year of college, I was so huge the only piece of clothing I owned that I could fit into was my pair of overalls. I was miserable about my size. The only variety in my wardrobe was to wear a different shirt under my overalls. In less than one year from the time I arrived at college, I had put on over thirty pounds.

Before my weight gain, I had done one national TV commercial back in Los Angeles from which I made several thousand dollars in residuals. Since my father was the highest paid stuntman in the business, during his prime, and my mother was a publicity writer for MGM Studios, I had connections in the motion picture industry. Because I was unfulfilled in college, I decided I would go back to Los Angeles, pursue a career in Hollywood, and make lots of money.

I returned home and did some "extra" (background people) work. It seemed like everyone, from directors and crew people to family and friends, told me the same embarrassing, humiliating line, which made me want to disappear and crawl under a rock where nobody could see me. "You have such a pretty face. If only you could lose some weight, you'd really go somewhere in this business." "Pleasingly plump" and "charmingly chubby" became all too common, embarrassing nicknames for me.

One day while I was working as an extra on the film *New York, New York,* I saw my first love, kissing and hugging his new girlfriend. She was beautiful—and thin! Now, I was determined to do anything to get that weight off, and I mean anything. I wanted to be thin and rich…and then I'd feel better about myself.

One day when I was working as an extra making sixty dollars a day, I watched a scene where a stuntwoman was pushed into a swimming pool. Later I learned that she made six hundred dollars that day. I thought, *Push me into the pool, please! I want to make six hundred dollars a day.* Also, I wanted everyone to applaud me like they did her; and all she had to do was splash into the water. That was the day I decided to become a stuntwoman. After all, with my dad and brother both being well-known stuntmen, I knew I had the connections I needed. My dad used to double Adam West on the *Batman* series, and my brother was also working steadily at that time. It was time to make some calls and put nepotism to work for me.

I still had one problem, however. I was too big to double for all those beautiful, slim actresses. *Why couldn't they just eat more ice cream and chocolate chip cookies?* I knew I had to get the weight off, so I started running, trying more diets, fasting for several days at a time, using diuretics and laxatives, throwing up my meals, taking pills to curb my appetite, and on and on. The rest is history. Before I knew what had hit me, I was a full-blown anorexic-bulimic on a slow road to destruction. Unfortunately, I couldn't see what was happening.

At age twenty-two I was slender enough to win a bikini

contest on the spur of the moment on the Santa Monica beach after becoming bored while watching my new boyfriend in his surfing contest. When he returned and saw me with my trophy and all kinds of prizes, he asked, "How did you win next to all those sixteen-year-old hard bodies?" That remark only left me feeling terrible, old, and ugly. I had to pull myself together. At least the judges thought I looked good, but I wondered why they voted for me. *I must have fooled them,* I thought at the time. I was holding in my stomach, and my tan must have made me look better than I really did. Well, I fooled them anyway. I fooled everybody! The truth was: I was feeling like the biggest, fattest, fool of all. Even though I looked good enough to win a bikini contest, I felt fat, ugly, and out of control. I desperately needed help.

Soon after, I checked into a health resort to try to get my eating disorder under control. I had read dozens of nutritional books in health food stores, so I knew what to do. I just couldn't do it. I felt helpless.

Over time, however, I did lose enough weight to be working. I was five feet seven inches tall and went up and down between 112 and 125 pounds; good enough to get a job in the film industry. My stunt career was taking off. I was doubling for Catherine Bach on *The Dukes of Hazzard* television series and I was on the road to getting "my way"—becoming rich and thin, that is. I came across to everyone as being happy-go-lucky, bubbly, and cheery. No one knew that on the inside I was insecure and unhappy. No one knew that I felt like I was dying.

I was now living a humiliating life in Manhattan Beach with a new alcoholic boyfriend who was beating me up on a regular basis, and I didn't want anyone to know about that either. When I first told this boyfriend I was moving out, he said he would kill himself and threw his head into a mirror. As blood rushed down his face, I remember thinking that I couldn't live with his death on my hands, so I stayed. As the relationship got worse, however, I knew I needed to get out. He knew his suicidal threat was no longer working, so when I tried to pack up my belongings, he locked me in a closet and threatened to kill me. Since I knew he was crazy enough to go through with killing me (and I wanted to live), I stayed with him and continued being emotionally and physically abused.

My self-image was at an all-time low. Life became so oppressing and depressing that I came to the point where I no longer cared if I lived or died. That was when I became brave enough to escape. If he killed me, so what? So, one day while he was gone I packed up and left. For the next several months I lived in hiding. I would move from one friend's house to the next as he continued to pound on their doors and even break into their homes. I felt like a worthless doormat. Everyone now knew I had been abused, which, in turn, made me feel like they thought very little of me for getting myself into a situation like that. In desperation, I began to cry out to God for help.

In the meantime, my career as a stuntwoman was beginning to soar. I got a theatrical agent and was doing acting roles as well. While attending one of my acting classes, I saw this good-looking, curly blond-haired man with muscular arms, and I immediately fell in love. I called my mom and said, "Mom, I met the man I'm going to marry." She said, "You're kidding. How long have you been going out with him?" I said, "I haven't gone out with him. He's not interested in me."

MAN OF MY DREAMS

You see, I looked pretty good on the outside and was wearing low-cut, high on the thigh, leopard-skin outfits to get his attention, but it wasn't working. I didn't understand why my get-ups were not turning his head my way. They had always worked with the other men I had wanted. As time passed, I found out that the man of my dreams was a born-again Christian and had been walking a straight path of celibacy for over two years.

Nightly, I dreamed about him, and in my dreams we were in love. His eyes would look at me as if he adored me. Then, I would go to acting class, and his eyes did nothing but look the other way. I still didn't get it, but I was determined to find out everything I could about him. Before long, I knew where he lived and where he worked.

One day out of the blue, one of my cousins called me and asked if I wanted to go to church with him. I inquired, "What kind of church?" He responded, "A Christian church." I immediately thought of Mel, the Christian man with the Bible who lived in Westwood and was always going to church; the Christian who I had my sights on marrying.

I asked, "Where is this church located?"

He answered, "Westwood."

I eagerly replied, "I'd love to go to church with you!"

I did go and was thrilled to find Mel at that very church, but there was more there than I had bargained for.

The beautiful music being played that day made me cry. It even *felt* like God was in that place. The pastor read from the Bible and talked about Jesus and about asking Him into your heart and making Him the Lord of your life. He also talked about the Holy Spirit. I knew I had to find out more.

When I went home that night I cried out to Jesus. I asked

Him to come into my heart. I immediately felt a peace that I had never felt before and I knew that everything was going to be all right. If you've never asked Jesus to come into your heart and to be the Lord of your life, I encourage you to do so right now. All you have to do is ask, and He will come into your heart and life. The peace of God will touch your heart, and not only will you feel like everything is going to be all right, it will happen, just like it did for me. Jesus will begin to lead and guide your life. He will give you wisdom and strength to make the right choices in your daily eating habits. Jesus will pick you up when you fall and show you loving kindness to help you start again. He will never give up on you.

Within six weeks from that time I was born-again, Spirit-filled, and married to the man of my dreams. Over twenty years later, Mel is not only the man of my dreams; he is exceedingly abundantly more than I could have ever hoped for or dreamed of in a husband!

Let me pause for a moment to explain that when you ask Jesus to come into your heart to be your Savior and Lord, you are born-again and when you leave earth at the end of your lifetime here, you will go to heaven. Before I became born-again, I didn't believe in heaven or hell. I believed that God is such a loving God that He would never send anyone to a place like hell. I did not understand that through that love He paved the way for us to be with Him eternally, but we have to receive that gift before we can receive its benefits.

While it is true that He is a loving God and does not want anyone to end up in hell, He also created us with a free will, the right to choose life with Him here on earth and for eternity. He tells us in His Word what to choose; choose life.

I encourage you to open your heart to Him now. Jesus said, "I am the way, the truth, and the life. No one comes to the Father except through Me" (John 14:6). The other doors are dead ends. I know. I've tried them.

New Beginnings

My new marriage was wonderful, but in some ways the honeymoon was very difficult. My grandmother gave us a trip to Europe as a wedding present, and Mel and I were together twenty-four hours a day. To top it off, Mel wanted to eat all the time. We would have a delicious dinner somewhere, but as soon as we walked out of the restaurant he'd want to go try out another place. This was a bulimic's nightmare. I didn't throw up my meals on our honeymoon for fear of him finding out and leaving me, so I came back from our honeymoon ten pounds heavier. I couldn't wait to get back to our home in Los Angeles where he would go to work and I could return to throwing up everything again.

After a couple of months of marriage, I broke down one night and cried, confessing my horrible sickness to him. The response was healing. Mel said, "Desiree, we are going to pray." *Well, that's great,* I thought. He said, "Go ahead." Well, I didn't know what to say or do. When it came to praying, all I had ever known to do was to pray silently like I had learned in the church I went to when I was growing up. My other point of reference was to cross my legs and chant like I had done when I was caught up in the New Age way of thinking.

Mel was expecting me to say something, but I sadly responded, "I don't know how to pray." Gently, he said, "That's OK, Desiree. I'll pray, and at the end you say, 'I agree.'" He then prayed the most beautiful prayer I had ever heard, and the peace of God filled my heart with hope as I said, "I agree."

I want to agree with you right now that the freedom and victory you are asking the Lord for in the area of your own eating disorder is yours in Jesus' name. I agree that you are set free in every area of your life and that you are walking in the fullness of life that God has for you.

The next morning I woke up with a strong desire to attend a local church in an area that I had never been to before. I phoned my girlfriend and she said she'd go with me. After the service started, the pastor called up a woman who looked like me. She was about my height and weight, and she shared how she was obsessed with working out, starving, and then throwing up her food. She called her condition bulimia. She then continued sharing about how Jesus had healed her. As she spoke, I cried like a baby. I knew the Lord had sent me there as the result of the prayer that Mel and I had prayed the night before. I also knew that if God had healed her, He could heal me, too. God is not a respecter of persons: what He had done for her, He would do for me; and what He has done for me, He will do for you!

That's why I am sharing my story with you. Jesus Christ set me completely free, and I have been walking in that victory for over twenty years. You and I don't have to stay bound. We can be free. I walked out of church that day knowing that I was healed. I was thrilled, but I had no idea then that I would experience the "slip" in less than a month's time.

KEEP YOUR EYES ON JESUS

Let me simply say that the next six months were a battle of life and death for me. At first I went around sharing the goodness of God with anyone who would listen. I returned to the church where I had heard the woman's testimony because they had a weekly support group for women with eating disorders. My husband encouraged me to attend so I could encourage the ladies by sharing about my healing. At that point it had been two whole weeks. The small group of ladies sat around in a circle as each lady shared graphic details of how much food they had eaten the previous week, starting with peanut butter and jelly sandwiches to malts and candy. The more they talked about the peanut butter, the hungrier I got. I also noticed that there seemed to be more talk about the ladies' problems than the solutions to those problems. Unfortunately, the room's atmosphere was heavy with despair and hopelessness.

"Where is the joyful woman who shared her testimony?" I asked one of the women. I was shocked when she said, "Oh, she's back in the hospital. We'll have to pray for her." Back in the hospital? But she testified that she was healed. What happened? One girl sadly replied that she had been in and out of the hospital several times. I wanted to go and pray for her and share how God had healed me.

When it was my turn to speak, I shared with the ladies that I was completely healed, but, no one rejoiced with me.

One lady asked, "For how long?"

I responded, "Two weeks."

"Yeah, right," someone said with a snicker. "So you had two weeks of abstinence! You don't get free of this kind of thing. You learn to live with it!" Someone from the group had died just a couple of months earlier and now our leader was in the hospital again with the same problem. My thunder was gone and I felt horrible. They continued talking about their food binges and purges for the next hour or so, and then we all prayed for the last five minutes that God would help us.

I learned some tough lessons in life at that time. One is that we are to keep our eyes on Jesus, not on people. Another is to realize that we become like those with whom we hang around. In Proverbs 4:23, the Word of God says, "Guard your heart, for it is the wellspring of life" (NIV). After attending a few more of those powerless meetings, I was back in my old cycle of binge-purge.

Even though I was again binging and purging, I wanted and needed to grow in my Christian walk. My God hunger was intense! I wanted more and more of Him, but at that time it seemed like nothing was working. I was both sad and angry. If this "Jesus thing" didn't work, then nothing would! He was my last chance. I was stuck in a rut that was leading to death—my death—but I cried out to God, "Please, help me!"

HEALED IN JESUS' NAME

Meanwhile, Mel was so proud of me and was telling others about my now-phony victory. I didn't want to tell him the truth because I was embarrassed and humiliated again. One day, however, I broke down while he was walking around the house, joyfully praising God, and sharing some revelation of victory he had received during a meeting he had attended.

I, on the other hand, was mad at everyone and everything. I was especially upset with him for being so joyful and victorious-sounding when I was stuck in this rut. *I'm going to let him have it!* I thought. I blurted out in tears and anger, "This faith stuff doesn't work! I tried it, and it doesn't work!" Shock and concern filled his face as he asked me what was wrong. In tears, I told him, "I'm throwing up my food again. I can't stop it. It doesn't work!" I will never forget the look in his eyes. It was like the fire of God coming out of him as he said, "Desiree, I don't care how many times you slip or how many times you fall, the Word of God says you are healed, and you are healed in Jesus' name!"

As he spoke those words, I felt life coming into my body. My head cleared. No longer did I see myself as a helpless victim of this horrible disease. I saw myself as an overcomer who had had a fall. If I fell, I could get back up and continue with a walk of victory. Hope was being restored as words of life were spoken over me. As Mel continued I could see and feel in the spirit realm. God's healing power shot through my body. Proverbs 18:21 says, "Death and life *are* in the power of the tongue." Life was being spoken over me. It was then that I got my first glimpse of who I really am in Christ—a healthy, beautiful, overcomer!

I came to understand that knowing who I really was according to God was the most critical key to my freedom. Was it a process? Yes. Were there challenges? Yes. But I have come to a place of complete victory, restoration, and peace through Jesus, and you can too! Next, I want to help you find out who you are in Christ. Once you realize your true identity, you can find victory in whatever circumstance, disease, disorder, or challenge you may be facing. You, too, can be an overcomer!

2

WHO TOLD YOU, YOU ARE FAT?

FROM MY EXPERIENCE as an anorexic-bulimic I began to realize that my eating disorder had started in my mind, and that the healing process would need to start there as well. In other words: I had to change my way of thinking.

At the time, my thoughts had been filled with goals of how much slimmer I would be by a certain date or event. I would stand on the scale several times a day, hoping to see that my weight had gone down. My mind was obsessed with my weight and with what I looked like. Even when I would starve myself for days on end and become very thin, I viewed myself as a heavy, overweight person.

One day a friend said to me, "Desiree, you are looking really good. Have you lost weight?" Instead of accepting her compliment, I replied, "Just look at my inner thighs and how flabby they are!" That example alone illustrates the fact that what I really needed was a change of mind regarding my self-image. I needed to find out how God thinks about me, how He sees me, and then I needed to align my own thinking about myself with His. I was looking at myself as a fat person. All it takes is one person calling you fat to see yourself in a negative light. God never calls us fat. He calls us perfect, being created in His image and likeness. We must listen to God's voice and not negative words from the past.

When I received Jesus as my Savior, I knew it would be possible for me to be free in my spirit, soul, and body. The more I focused on Him rather than on myself, the more freedom I experienced. I began to find out through reading the Bible that God loves me and finds me precious and beautiful to behold.

God loves you, too, and feels the same way about you. You were created by Him. You are one of a kind and very special. You're a part of Him. You are His precious child, and you, too, are beautiful to behold. That's the truth!

Understanding who you really are is crucial to obtaining your healthy body weight and your peace of mind. You may be wondering what this understanding has to do with losing or gaining weight. I believe your body is a reflection of your spirit. Show me a person with an eating disorder and I'll show you someone with low self-esteem. Once we begin to eliminate our low self-esteem, the rest will follow. The Bible puts it this way: "For as he [or she] thinks in his [or her] heart, so is he [or she]" (Proverbs 23:7).

WHAT GOD'S WORD SAYS ABOUT WHO YOU ARE

I began to earnestly read the Bible, looking for scriptures that would help me with what I was going through. When I did this, I found that God has quite a bit to say about food and eating. My first scripture to freedom was Matthew 4:4: "Man shall not live by bread alone, but by every word that proceeds from the mouth of God!"

Soon, I found other verses such as:

> Therefore I tell you, do not worry about your life, what
> you will eat or drink; or about your body, what you
> will wear. Is not life more important than food, and
> the body more important than clothes?
> —MATTHEW 6:25, NIV

> I am the bread of life. He who comes to Me shall never
> hunger, and he who believes in Me shall never thirst.
> —JOHN 6:35

Daily I continued reading the Word of God and spending time with Jesus. Many scriptures touched me, and as I read them I underlined them in my Bible and wrote them down in a journal. Interestingly, as I spoke the scriptures out loud and meditated on them, my physical appetite started coming under control and I began to experience deep healing in my heart and mind. My mind was being renewed by the Word of God. It was being filled with good things—with life, health, and healing. I realized I was more than a physical body, and I was finding out who I was in Christ. I was God's daughter, dearly loved by Him, and He was always with me to help me in every way.

I do remember what it had been like to feel there was no possible way I could ever lose weight or look the way I thought I should. Like many of you, I had tried every diet, been through every exercise program, and had bought countless items that promised to help me lose weight; all to no avail. I can tell you today, however, the one road to true, lasting victory in this area of eating disorders, and in every area of life, lies with God alone! As you and I begin to understand how He really sees us, we can see ourselves correctly and our bodies will line up with what we believe.

My prayer is that you will begin to get a true revelation of what a unique, beautiful, and powerful glory-house you really are. When this happens, control over your eating habits and attaining a healthy weight can become reality for you.

What I'm going to share with you is what set me completely free from a negative self-image, free from an unhealthy lifestyle, and free to become my best self. As you receive and act on the following truth, God can heal you of your eating disorder and will use you to help others. You, dear friend, are a powerhouse vessel for God. Go for it! You can do it!

Let's begin with what God says about you. First of all, you are like the Lord. You are one with Him. How can this be? Well, just think for a moment how awesome God is. He's the Creator of heaven and earth—and of everyone. Can you imagine what His child would be like? Like Him, of course. And that's you! In Genesis 1:26 we read: "Then God said, 'Let Us make man in Our image, according to Our likeness.'"

Now, how do you become His child? When you ask Him to be your Savior and Lord, you become spiritually born again and you become His child.

I think the following verse is so comforting: "Behold what manner of love the Father has bestowed on us, that we should be called children of God!" (1 John 3:1). It's as if the writer knew some of us might struggle with this idea, so he reminds us of it because he wants to be sure we understand. The truth is, we really are His children. Little children grow up to be adults like their parents, right? So then, as we grow spiritually, we become like our heavenly Father who is God.

As I mentioned earlier, most people with eating disorders suffer from low self-esteem. But as a child of God, it's not His plan for you to see yourself lower than He created you. He created you perfectly in His image. When you ask Jesus to be your Savior and Lord, then you are His child. But we are all also in a life-long process of becoming like Him. While we're still on this planet, no one will fully "arrive" at the point of being just like Him. We are all works in progress. And as we continue to spend time with Him, in His Word and in prayer, He gives us the power by His Holy Spirit to change. In Philippians 1:6, we read: "He who has begun a good work in you will complete it until the day of Jesus Christ."

Throughout our lives we are being molded into His image. Romans 8:29 says that we are "predestined to be conformed to the image of [Christ]." The Amplified translation reads, "He also destined from the beginning [foreordaining them] to be molded into the image of His Son [and share inwardly His likeness]."

As Jesus prayed to the Father, He spoke of those who follow Him as being one with Him, as being part of Him, even as He is part of the Father. And He declares that the glory of the Lord is upon us!

> And all Mine are Yours, and Yours are Mine, and I am glorified in them. Now I am no longer in the world, but these are in the world, and I come to You. Holy Father, keep through Your name those whom You have given Me, that they may be one as We are.
> —JOHN 17:10–11

> I do not pray for these alone, but also for those who will believe in Me through their word; that they all

> may be one, as You, Father, are in Me, and I in You;
> that they also may be one in Us, that the world may
> believe that You sent Me. And the glory which You
> gave Me I have given them, that they may be one just
> as We are one.
>
> —JOHN 17:20–22

We also see we are dearly loved by our Father and that His love is in us!

> I in them, and You in Me; that they may be made per-
> fect in one, and that the world may know that You
> have sent Me, and have loved them as You have loved
> Me. "Father, I desire that they also whom You gave
> Me may be with Me where I am, that they may behold
> My glory which You have given Me; for You loved
> Me before the foundation of the world….And I have
> declared to them Your name, and will declare it, that
> the love with which You loved Me may be in them,
> and I in them."
>
> —JOHN 17: 23–24, 26

What great news this is. You are one with the Lord! The glory of the Lord is upon you. You are loved by the Father, and His love is in you. Can you begin to see how precious and powerful you really are? Believe what His Word says about you!

Now let's look at some steps on the road to an overcomer's life, a powerful life of freedom and peace.

MAKE A DECISION TO THINK TRUE THOUGHTS

Everything begins with a thought. Our thoughts are who we are and who we will become. So, thinking correctly is crucial for our lives. In Proverbs 23:7, King Solomon said,

"For as he [a person] thinks in his heart, so is he."

In terms of breaking free from my eating disorder, I recognized that my thoughts had been limited and had been full of self-condemnation. What I believed about myself and about my future had been based upon what people around me said. Unfortunately, the person around me most was my alcoholic boyfriend who was demeaning and abusive.

At the same time, I was working hard to break into the entertainment business, so I frequently compared myself harshly with other performers or with what the casting directors were calling for. Internally, I was obsessed with my appearance and started starving myself. Then, I'd be so hungry that I'd eat lots of food. After that, out of guilt and the fear of weight gain, I'd make myself throw up everything I had just eaten. This is how anorexia and bulimia works.

I did get down to a much smaller size, but I also became physically sick from all the starvation, binging, and purging. And the effects were not only physical. My very being hurt and I knew I had to get help. I longed to be free from negative thoughts, from the pressure of comparison, from my feelings of insecurity, and from the fear that someone would discover what was really going on with me. The day finally came when I cried out to God and He helped me!

I'll share a few keys He showed me that brought me victory in the area of thinking.

First of all, I learned to push away or cast down any thought or word that came against or contradicted God's Word. In 2 Corinthians 10:5, God tells us: "Casting down arguments and every high thing that exalts itself against the knowledge of God, bringing every thought into captivity to the obedience of Christ."

You have the power and ability to do just that. Remember,

you are a powerhouse for God. His very presence is on the inside of you. With Him on your side and within you, you win! So make the decision—and, yes, it's a decision—to push away or cast down bad thoughts or terrible things anyone has said to you or about you. God will help you do this!

The next key is to get hooked up and stay hooked up to God's Word. As I began to discover in the Bible all He says about me, I was blessed with peace and joy. I've found that God's Word is true, alive, and full of hope. Because God is truth and He is love, there is power in Him and in His Word to set us free. Jesus said:

> If you abide in My word [hold fast to My teachings and live in accordance with them], you are truly My disciples. And you will know the Truth, and the Truth will set you free.
> —JOHN 8:31–32, AMP

He also said:

> I am the way, the truth, and the life.
> —JOHN 14:6

Because Jesus is with us and within us, you and I can have complete victory in our thoughts over negativity, distorted thinking, and temptation. He has promised to help, by the power of the Holy Spirit, when we ask Him to do so.

Finally, as you discover and receive all the good and positive truths the Lord says about you, I encourage you to dwell on them in the way Philippians 4:8 tells us that we are to do:

> Finally, brethren, whatever things are true, whatever things are noble, whatever things are just, whatever

things are pure, whatever things are lovely, whatever things are of good report, if there is any virtue and if there is anything praiseworthy—meditate on these things.

Does this mean we live in a bubble or with our heads in the sand? No. But it does mean we choose to think thoughts of life and healing rather than to continue to replay the dramas or trials of life we may be facing. We can choose to find and focus on the positive. We can think of ourselves as thin. We can choose to continually think the best of ourselves; to think in our favor! When you think of you, think of you at your perfect weight. What do you look like? What do you feel like? From there, act like you are already at that perfect weight.

Since God's Word is alive and will transform whatever it is applied to—in both the spiritual and physical realms—choose to learn His Word and ways and to think true thoughts: His thoughts!

A NEW CREATION

You are God's precious child. He paid an outrageous price for you and for the authority you carry. You are, after all, a beautiful, walking powerhouse with unlimited potential. To know how precious you are, you need to understand how precious He is. To know who you are, you need to know who He is and to truly understand all He's done for you! And one of the things the Word says about you is that you are a new creation. In 2 Corinthians 5:17, we read:

Therefore, if anyone is in Christ, he is a new creation; old things have passed away; behold, all things have become new.

The Amplified version reads:

> Therefore if any person is [ingrafted] in Christ (the Messiah) he is a new creation (a new creation altogether); the old [previous moral and spiritual condition] has passed away. Behold, the fresh and new has come!

Isn't that wonderful news? Your past is severed; you are brand new! What a great way to begin each day, knowing that you're new, knowing that He's in you and with you to help you grow and change and become all you can be. From 2 Corinthians 3:18, we learn: "But we all, with unveiled face, beholding as in a mirror the glory of the Lord, are being transformed into the same image from glory to glory, just as by the Spirit of the Lord." But you have a part to play in the process of transformation. You must be willing to change and be transformed.

Don't be like the caterpillar in this next story: Two caterpillars were crawling through the grass when a butterfly flew over them. When the caterpillars looked up, one nudged the other and said, "You couldn't get me up in one of those things for a million dollars!" Obviously, he was afraid. But, the caterpillar's destiny was to fly. You, too, have a wonderful destiny to fulfill. Don't be afraid to step out into it. There's an amazing plan of God for you to walk in and enjoy. He wants to bless you and He wants you to be a blessing to others. Remember, you've been made new.

YOU ARE NOT ALONE IN THIS BATTLE

God is with you. He is on your side. And He fights for you. Hebrews 13:5 tells us:

... He [God] Himself has said, I will not in any way fail you nor give you up nor leave you without support. [I will] not, [I will] not, [I will] not in any degree leave you helpless nor forsake nor let [you] down (relax My hold on you)! [Assuredly not!]

—AMP

I also love what 2 Chronicles 16:9 says:

For the eyes of the LORD run to and fro throughout the whole earth, to show Himself strong on behalf of those whose heart is loyal to Him.

What do you need in your life right now? What do you need in order to be healthy, to be at your best body weight? If you are anorexic or bulimic, do you need to gain some weight to be within a healthy range? Conversely, are you overweight or obese? You can lose the extra 10, 20, 100, or whatever pounds you need to lose. Jesus Christ will help you. God cares. He has every hair on your head numbered. He knows how much you weigh, how much you want to weigh, and the healthiest weight for you.

YOU REALLY CAN

Because you can, learn to say the words, *I can*. Clear your mind of the words, *I can't*. There is no failure except in not trying. Triumph is just *umph* added to *try*. You need to be speaking God's Word and speaking life over yourself at all times. You need to build up the things of God in your life.

He is our source of strength and provides whatever we need to become successful, but we need to do our part as well. We need to choose right thoughts, speak them out loud over ourselves, and take action to train our flesh.

31

Remember, it's a partnership. The Holy Spirit is not the doer; the Word of God says He is the Helper that will help us when we call on Him. There's really nothing that can stop us when we partner with God.

When I was a little girl, I wasn't allowed to say the word *can't*. In fact, I got spanked if I said the "can't" word. Now, I'm so thankful that "can't" was not part of my upbringing and I was taught to think that I could do anything. I believe that was key to my becoming one of Hollywood's top working stuntwomen. A woman who liked to have manicures, pedicures, and spa time, and who also had a serious fear of heights and high falls, was able to do high falls fearlessly and with a heart full of joy. How was that possible? I believed I could. I didn't use the word "can't" when it came to my work.

My dad, who was also in the stunt business, taught me well. To learn how to do high falls, he took me up a 30-foot ladder to jump onto an airbag. One step at a time, on each consecutive rung of the ladder, with each consecutive jump, he had me confess 2 Timothy 1:7: "For God has not given us a spirit of fear, but of power and of love and of a sound mind." In less than an hour, I was having a blast at the top of the ladder, jumping off into the air and landing perfectly.

Later in my life, in the ministry, applying the same Bible principles of "I can do all things through Christ" and acknowledging that He has given me His power, love, and a sound mind has helped me to live in peace and victory and to do great things for His glory (Phil. 4:13). God will be delighted to help you in the same manner. You just need to ask Him, believe that He will help you, and then do what He shows you to do; not only in the area of your eating, but in every area of your life. Remember, you are not alone!

Focus On Him, Not On Your Body Weight

One of the challenges someone with an eating disorder faces is an unbalanced or unhealthy relationship with food and/or an obsession with body weight. Let's face it, food is not illegal. It can be delicious and healthy, and we need it to live. It's not like you can pray or say, "Well, I'm just never going to touch food again," like you can with drugs, alcohol, or smoking. We all need to eat. However, with an eating disorder, things are out of balance, even to the point of addiction. The reason for this is we focus on the wrong things. Instead of focusing on God and all He has for us, we focus on ourselves, on our bodies, and on food itself.

Here's another key to healing, to balance, and to overcoming any addiction. It's simply this: take your eyes off the challenge, off the food, and off yourself, and put your eyes on Jesus! Truly, this is a heart trust issue, but it's one that God is completely committed to helping us to do.

Know the One You Love

Where do you fix your attention? How do you spend your time? Do you love Jesus? If you do, then you need to know Him and spend time with Him. After all, when we love someone, we want to be with that person, don't we? We talk to the other person so that they can learn about us and we listen so that we can learn about them. If I call my husband on the phone and try to joke around with him, pretending I'm someone else, he always knows it's me. Why? Because we spend time together, we talk with one another. He knows me. We've been married over twenty years. We know each other!

As we continue to spend time with those we love, we begin to pick up some of their mannerisms. We might start to think like they do, use some of their phrases or jokes, or respond to situations the way they do. Mel has always said that the five people closest to you are the ones you are like. And it's true. I've watched it happen in me, and I've seen it with my son and his friends. As parents, aren't we careful about with whom our children hang around? Why is that? It's because those you spend time with influence you. Some of my friends are very funny. I like to have fun, so I enjoy hanging out with them. And as I do, I find my own heart lifted as we spend time together. We end up taking a little of each other's joy with us as we go our own way.

The same is true about our love-walk with God. When I keep my eyes on the Lord and when I spend time with Him, I become like Him. What's on Him gets on me, and I'm transformed by being in His presence!

I want to talk a little more about the importance and power of our focus. Hebrews 12:1–2 tells us to "lay aside every weight." (You see, the Bible does talk about how to lose weight!) The same verse tells us how to run:

> Therefore we also, since we are surrounded by so great a cloud of witnesses, let us lay aside every weight, and the sin which so easily ensnares us, and let us run with endurance the race that is set before us, looking unto Jesus, the author and finisher of our faith, who for the joy that was set before Him endured the cross, despising the shame, and has sat down at the right hand of the throne of God.

We are to run our race (the course of our life here on earth) with endurance, looking unto Jesus! We are to focus our eyes on Him.

Focus, focus, focus! Ask any athlete about it. I used to run marathon races and I can tell you that focus is absolutely critical. As you train properly, your endurance increases and you are strengthened. But no matter how much you've trained, running twenty-six miles is pushing your body to an extreme. In order to complete your race, in order to win, you must focus on finishing the race; you must focus on the prize. That's how you break through the proverbial "wall" when you hit it; that's where you get your second wind when you need it. You focus on the prize.

In our walk as believers, and especially in breaking addictions and living free and peacefully, we, too, need to keep our eyes on the prize. The key is to keep our eyes on Jesus.

Remember, your focus determines the direction you will go. There's hope. Don't quit. You will win if you don't give up! I love what the Word says in Colossians 1:27: "Christ in you, the hope of glory." Look to your power source! As you focus on God and as you are in His presence, you will be transformed and you will be victorious!

THE REAL YOU MUST TAKE YOUR PLACE

The real you is a powerhouse for the glory of God. Do you believe that? There is so much God on the inside of you that is alive and can accomplish anything godly that you desire. But you must receive that in your heart and then act like it is true. God will not make you accomplish the things you desire. He will certainly help you with it every step of the way. After all, as a believer you are His child, created in His image and likeness. That's who we are, and we must start to act like what we are.

Look at some of the things He tells us in His Word about who we are, about our function, and about the power He has given us to live:

🌱 We are crowned with glory and honor (Ps. 8:5).

🌱 We are the light of the world (Matt. 5:14).

🌱 We are more than conquerors through Him who loved us (Rom. 8:37).

🌱 We are strengthened with might through His Spirit (Eph. 3:16).

God has given each one of us what we need to carry out the assignments He has for us:

🌱 He gives us a new heart; one capable of hearing and responding to Him (Ezek. 11:19).

🌱 He expects us to share the life He has so generously given us and He gives us the power to totally get rid of anything that would stand in the way of that (Matt. 10:1–8).

🌱 He gives us His authority to do what He asks us to and He gives us His protection along with it (Luke 10:19; 1 John 5:18).

🌱 He supplies all our needs (Philippians 4:19).

Is it any wonder that our enemy Satan would come against us so hard to try to distort the truth about our inner image or about who we are in Christ? The devil is terrified that if we really get a hold of this truth, we'll walk in victory in every area of our lives. Then, we'll become lighthouses for others to get free of whatever it is that's harming them or holding them back from who they truly are.

The enemy is terrified of believers who know who they are

in Christ, those who are growing in their spiritual maturity and living in Christian victory, those who do great works for God...including passing that life on to others in the body of Christ. So, Satan wars against us. He wants to destroy us before we can destroy his dark and evil works. The Bible doesn't say we won't have challenges, but God does promise that He will be with us and that He "will never leave [us] nor forsake [us]" (Heb. 13:5). We can come through each test, each trial, and each of life's challenges victorious!

> You are of God, little children, and have overcome them, because He who is in you is greater than he who is in the world.
>
> —1 JOHN 4:4

> For whatever is born of God overcomes the world. And this is the victory that has overcome the world—our faith.
>
> —1 JOHN 5:4

> But if the Spirit of Him who raised Jesus from the dead dwells in you, He who raised Christ from the dead will also give life to your mortal bodies through His Spirit who dwells in you.
>
> —ROMANS 8:11

This verse in Romans is saying that the same Holy Spirit that raised Jesus from the dead is alive inside of you and me. Why? To empower us as God's children to live in the fullness of life that He has for us and to share this life with others. Jesus told His followers:

> Most assuredly, I say to you, he who believes in Me, the works that I do he will do also; and greater works

than these he will do, because I go to My Father.

—JOHN 14:12

I encourage you and challenge you to rise up and take your place as God's victorious child. Then help someone else to know the truth and freedom that comes from being God's child!

DECLARE THE TRUTH ABOUT YOURSELF

The following is a detailed list of loving, hope-filled, powerful words God says about us as His children. I recommend that you copy and keep this list in a place where you will see it daily (like in your planner, somewhere in your bathroom, near your mirror, or someplace where you will see it often). Take it out, read it, and speak it out loud over yourself. Let the Word of God, which is alive and powerful, do its work in your life today.

WHO I AM IN CHRIST

- ❧ I am God's child, for I am born-again of the incorruptible seed of "the word of God which lives and abides forever" (1 Pet. 1:23).

- ❧ I am forgiven of all my sins and washed in the Blood (Eph. 1:7; Heb. 9:14; Col. 1:14).

- ❧ I am a new creature (2 Cor. 5:17).

- ❧ I am the temple of the Holy Spirit (1 Cor. 6:19).

- ❧ I am delivered from the power of darkness and translated into God's kingdom (Col. 1:13).

❦ I am redeemed from the curse of the law (Gal. 3:13).

❦ I am blessed (Deut. 28:1–14; Gal. 3:9).

❦ I am a saint (Rom. 1:7; 1 Cor. 1:2; Phil. 1:1).

❦ I am "the head and not the tail... above only, and not... beneath" (Deut. 28:13).

❦ I am "holy and without blame before Him in love" (Eph. 1:4).

❦ I am the elect (Col. 3:12).

❦ I am confirmed and established to the end (1 Cor. 1:8).

❦ I am brought near to God by the blood of Christ (Eph. 2:13).

❦ I am victorious (1 John 5:4).

❦ I am set free (John 8:31–33).

❦ I am strong in the Lord (Eph. 6:10).

❦ I am dead to sin (Rom. 6:2,11; 1 Pet. 2:24).

❦ I am more than a conqueror (Rom. 8:37).

❦ I am a joint heir with Christ (Rom. 8:17).

❦ I am "sealed with the Holy Spirit of promise" (Eph. 1:13).

❦ I am in Christ Jesus by His doing (1 Cor. 1:30).

❦ I am "accepted in the Beloved" (Eph. 1:6).

❦ I am "complete in Him" (Col. 2:10).

❦ I am "crucified with Christ" (Gal. 2:20).

❦ I am free from condemnation (Rom. 8:1).

❦ I am reconciled to God (Col. 1:20).

❦ I am qualified to share in His inheritance
(Col. 1:12).

❦ I am firmly rooted, built up, established in my
faith, and overflowing with gratitude (Col. 2:7).

❦ I am a fellow citizen with the saints and of the
household of God (Eph. 2:19).

❦ I am "built on the foundation of the apostles and
prophets, Jesus Christ Himself being the chief
corner stone" (Eph. 2:20).

❦ I am in the world as He is in heaven (1 John 4:17).

❦ I am born of God and the evil one does not touch
me (1 John 5:18).

❦ I am His faithful follower (Rev. 17:14).

❦ I am overtaken with blessings (Deut. 28:2; Eph. 1:3).

❦ I am His disciple because I have love for others
(John 13:34– 35).

❦ I am the salt of the earth and the light of the world
(Matt. 5:13–14).

🍂 I am the righteousness of God in Christ Jesus (2 Cor. 5:21).

🍂 I am a partaker of His divine nature (2 Pet. 1:4).

🍂 I am called of God (2 Tim. 1:9).

🍂 I am the firstfruits among His creation (James 1:18).

🍂 I am chosen (1 Thess. 1:4; Eph. 1:4; 1 Pet. 2:9).

🍂 I am an ambassador for Christ (2 Cor. 5:20).

🍂 I am God's "workmanship, created in Christ Jesus for good works" (Eph. 2:10).

🍂 I am the apple of my Father's eye (Deut. 32:10; Ps. 17:8).

🍂 I am healed by the stripes of Jesus (Isa. 53:5; 1 Pet. 2:24).

🍂 I am being changed into His image (2 Cor. 3:18).

🍂 I am raised up with Christ and seated in heavenly places (Eph. 2:6).

🍂 I am beloved of God (Rom. 1:7).

🍂 I am one in Christ (John 17:21–23).

🍂 I have the mind of Christ (Phil. 2:5; 1 Cor. 2:16).

🍂 I have obtained an inheritance (Eph. 1:11).

🍂 I "have access by one Spirit to the Father" (Eph. 2:18).

🌱 I have overcome the world (1 John 5:4).

🌱 I have everlasting life and will not be condemned (John 5:24; John 6:47).

🌱 I have "the peace of God, which surpasses all understanding" (Phil. 4:7).

🌱 I have received the power of the Holy Spirit to lay hands on the sick and see them recover, the power to cast out demons, power over the enemy, and nothing shall by any means hurt me (Mark 16:17–18).

🌱 I live by and in "the law of the Spirit of life in Christ Jesus" (Rom. 8:2).

🌱 I walk in Christ Jesus (Col. 2:6).

🌱 I can do all things through Christ Jesus (Phil. 4:13).

🌱 I shall do even greater works than these in Christ Jesus (John 14:12).

🌱 I possess the greater One in me, because greater is He who is in me than he who is in the world (1 John 4:4).

🌱 I press toward the mark for the prize of the high calling of God (Phil. 3:14).

🌱 I always triumph in Christ (2 Cor. 2:14).

🌱 I show forth His praise (1 Pet. 2:9).

🌱 My "life is hidden with Christ in God" (Col. 3:3).

God is not finished with you. In Philippians 1:6, He says, "Being confident of this very thing, that He who has begun a good work in you will complete it until the day of Jesus Christ." God will help you. He will see you through whatever challenges you're facing today.

Daily, pray this simple prayer:

> *Father, help me to see myself as You see me. I can weigh my perfect weight in Jesus' name. Use me to be a vessel of your blessing here on earth. I speak strength to my body. Body, I command you to work perfectly in Jesus' name. Digestive system: speed up in Jesus name; elimination system: work perfectly in Jesus' name. Body: weigh your perfect weight in Jesus' name. I exercise physically. I eat good foods, the right portions at the right time of day. Father, thank You for helping me to exercise self-control. I submit myself to You. I resist the devil in every way. I resist wrong foods in Jesus' name. I am more than a conqueror. You keep me in perfect peace as I choose to keep my eyes on You. Lord, thank You for loving me and thank You for empowering me to succeed. I can do all things through Christ, the anointed One, and His anointing, which strengthens me! Amen.*

God loves you so very much and has a wonderful plan and purpose for your life. I encourage you to embrace the truth about yourself. Live in the fullness of all He has for you and pass it on to others.

Read these words by Marianne Williamson:[1]

> Our deepest fear is not that we are inadequate. Our deepest fear is that we are powerful beyond measure. It is our light, not our darkness that most frightens us. We ask ourselves, "Who am I to be brilliant, gorgeous,

talented, and fabulous?" Actually, who are you not to be? You are a child of God. Your playing small doesn't serve the world. There's nothing enlightened about shrinking so that other people won't feel insecure around you. We were born to manifest the glory of God that is within us...And as we let our light shine, we unconsciously give other people permission to do the same. As we are liberated from our own fear, our presence automatically liberates others.

3

WRITE IT, READ IT, AND RUN

T

O HELP GAIN victory over any eating disorder, you must identify and clearly state your personal visions and goals. In other words, set a course and make a plan for your life.

It's been said that those who fail to plan, plan to fail. Not that people set out to fail, but the Bible says that even God's own children can be destroyed for a lack of knowledge. (See Hosea 4:6.) I'm going to share several steps in this chapter that can set you on course and keep you moving forward, keys that can produce tremendous fruit in your life as you heed the information and take action.

1. Vision—Discovering your heart's desires

What is vision? Certainly, we know that vision is the power of seeing with the human eye. Vision is also something perceived in a dream or in a trance. It can be something supernaturally revealed, as to a prophet. It can be a mental image, the ability to perceive something not actually visible, as through keen foresight. It can be a force or power of the imagination. Vision is a precious, God-given gift given to each one of us to see and to imagine what our future might hold.

The devil tries to pervert your vision with fear or doubt, or by presenting you with other images—negative ones. That's why it's so important that you flood your mind with God's Word, which produces godly visions and goals. Proverbs 29:18 says, "Where there is no vision [no redemptive revelation of God], the people perish" (AMP). Do not let your dreams, purpose, and God-given desires perish simply because of a lack of vision for your life.

The first step is to identify the vision God has given you. How do you know for sure that your visions and dreams are from God? You know by spending time with Him in His Word and in prayer. Again, when you spend time with someone, you begin to know the sound of the person's voice. You can anticipate his/her words and actions because you really know the person. The same holds true in our walk with God.

God has a glorious plan for you. (See Jeremiah 29:11.) You're His child, and as such you have the potential to become a world shaker and a history-maker. In His Word He says that He wants to do exceedingly abundantly above anything you could think, hope, or ask for. (See Ephesians 3:20.) So just imagine right now the greatest plan you could have for your life. God wants to do even more than that for you and through you, for His glory and your benefit!

Next, spend some time thinking. In other words, take time to dream. If money were no object, if time was not an issue, if you could wake up in the morning and do anything or go anywhere, what or where would that be? What kind of person would you be? How would you spend your private time? How would you spend your family, work, church, friends', and public time?

What would you look like? Really, what would you look like? How much would you weigh? How would you dress? How active would you be? What would your energy level be like? Would you be strong? What does strong, healthy, and beautiful look like to you? Ask the Lord for clarification and for direction in all of these areas. But, also allow yourself to be real. What do you really want? What does God have to say about it all? Don't be intimidated and don't be anxious. God can handle your dreams and your requests. Philippians 4:6 says:

> Do not fret or have any anxiety about anything, but in every circumstance and in everything, by prayer and petition (definite requests), with thanksgiving, continue to make your wants known to God.
>
> —AMP

I love that: "with thanksgiving." That means you believe that God is going to get involved, that God's going to help you. Now that's faith!

2. Write down your goals.

Next, it's important for you to write down your goals and visions, your desires and dreams.

> Write the vision and make it plain on tablets, that he may run who reads it. For the vision is yet for an appointed time; but at the end it will speak, and it will not lie. Though it tarries, wait for it; because it will surely come, it will not tarry.
>
> —HABAKKUK 2:2–3

Write down the things that you want to come to pass the rest of this year, next year, or sometime in your future. Ask God to give you clear vision of all of these things. He already knows, but it's a point of contact for you and Him. You're in this together. Besides, when you write it down, it helps you to focus and set goals. It helps you to take the small, day-by-day steps necessary to attain your dreams. If you don't know where you're going, that's exactly where you'll end up!

The dictionary defines *goal* as an object or an end that you strive to attain. I like how Hebrews 11:1 defines it:

> Now faith is the substance of things hoped for, the evidence of things not seen.

Goal-setting is part of faith. It's something you believe for. That's why it works whether you're saved or you're not saved. God's kingdom principles work for whoever will apply them. When you write down a goal, you release the supernatural power of God to get involved and you see that which you have written become a reality in your life.

Psalms 20:4 says, "May He grant you according to your heart's desire, And fulfill all your purpose." I love that scripture. And this is my prayer for you: "May God grant you your heart's desire and fulfill all your plans!" But first you must make a plan. Write it down. Be specific about what you want for your life. You get one shot at living on Planet Earth. One day you're twenty years old, then thirty, then forty, then fifty, sixty, and so on! It's just amazing how fast the years fly by. How do you want to live your life? Healthy? Satisfied? Significant?

3. Take action!

Step three is to take action. Once you've discovered and

know your goals and visions, and are focused enough to have written them down, you must do something about achieving your goals. You have to press. You have to work. You have to put your hands to something!

> I press toward the goal for the prize of the upward call of God in Christ Jesus.
> —Philippians 3:14

Part of taking action and moving forward includes counting the cost. The question to ask yourself is: do I really want to do what it takes to accomplish this goal? A lot of people think they want to run a marathon, but how much do they really want to do it? To finish the race of running a marathon (26 miles), it takes training and prep work months ahead of time. It's running 10 miles, 15 miles, 20 miles, all the way up to 70 miles a week. It's intense and it takes discipline. But that's true with anything worth having or accomplishing.

The same applies to attaining a healthy weight and good eating habits. The good news with this, however, is that God is clearly committed to helping you with it. In 3 John 1:2, He says, "Beloved, I pray that you may prosper in all things and be in health, just as your soul prospers." It's His heartfelt desire that you be in good health, and that includes you being at an appropriate weight. Nonetheless, it's a partnership, and one of the things you must do is count the cost as you begin to take action.

Do you really want to feel, look, and be healthy, strong, and at the weight that's right for you? I believe you do! What will that mean for you? Will it take cutting back on the number of lattés you drink weekly? Will it take no more eating ice cream late at night? Does the very word exercise make you tired? How about starting to walk during your lunch break a few times a week? Taking little steps consistently over a period of time is a good place to start. It encourages you to start taking the bigger steps that are also necessary to succeed.

In James 2:20, we see that God is serious about our active participation: "Faith without works is dead." That means that you can't sit at home and eat chocolate fudge all day long while proclaiming, "I weigh 120 pounds, in Jesus' name! Yes, I weigh 120 pounds!" No, you don't. In this case, your faith has no works to go with it. Put the fudge down and begin to eat healthy foods. Exercise. Otherwise, you can have faith to be 120 pounds, but your faith is dead if you are not doing your part.

Be a person of great faith, not one who is flaky, irresponsible, and not putting their hand to the plow to work. Take action on what you're trying to accomplish. Be faithful, and then you will see your rewards for your faithful action.

> His lord said to him, 'Well done, good and faithful servant; you were faithful over a few things, I will make you ruler over many things. Enter into the joy of your lord.'
>
> —MATTHEW 25:21

Every step of the way God is with you, and each small success builds upon the other until you achieve the greater success. Faithful with little, ruler over much!

Another benefit of setting goals and taking action is that it severs or releases you from your past and propels you into your divine destiny. I want you to see this in the Word so that you will be excited about and consumed with fulfilling your goals. I want you to be filled with joy over the idea that you're going to accomplish great things in the area of attaining a victorious lifestyle. Philippians 3:13 says:

> Brethren, I do not count myself to have apprehended; but one thing I do, forgetting those things which are behind and reaching forward to those things which are ahead.

In the Amplified translation it reads, "Straining forward to what lies ahead." That's what goal-setting does. It pushes you forward and lets you see your destiny. As you let go of the past and focus on the future, it helps you run your race to the mark of your high calling in Christ Jesus.

4. Speak your goals out loud.

Step four is to speak your goals out loud. The ten wealthiest people in the United States all had one thing in common: goal-setting. The top five wealthiest people had something else in common: they spoke out their goals daily. Proverbs 18:21 says, "Death and life are in the power of the tongue." What a powerful scripture this is. It implies that we create our future by the words we speak. This works both in the positive and in the negative. Have you ever been around people who speak negatively most of the time; who complain, gossip, or criticize? When you hear what comes out of their mouths, there's nothing constructive; there's no life, no hope in any of it. Maybe you've even been that way yourself. Even so, when you hear this kind of dialog, you know it isn't right. There's something about it that grieves your spirit.

My advice is to not answer in like manner. Rather than scolding someone for saying something negative, replace it with something positive. Focusing on the positive is a much healthier way to live. The same holds true with what drives or motivates you. Get consumed with your divine destiny. Faithfully speak life over all your situations.

> For assuredly, I say to you, whoever says to this mountain, "Be removed and be cast into the sea," and does not doubt in his heart, but believes that those things he says will be done, he will have whatever he says.
> —MARK 11:23

5. Empower your goals with the Word of God.

Step five is to empower your goals with the Word of God. You do this because the Word is Jesus and it is powerful. (See John 1:1.) You want to bring Jesus into everything you're doing.

> So then faith comes by hearing, and hearing by the word of God.
> —ROMANS 10:17

If you hear your goal spoken with the Word of God, then supernatural power and faith cover your goal and will bring it to pass. It says in Hebrews 4:12:

> For the word of God is living and powerful, and sharper than any two-edged sword, piercing even to the division of soul and spirit, and of joints and marrow, and is a discerner of the thoughts and intents of the heart.

Make it a priority to put the Word into everything that you do.

6. Prioritize—Set your first goal.

Step six is to begin by setting your first goal. I want to suggest that this is easier than it may seem. For those of you who have never done any goal-setting in your life, it's vital that you first start with you and God.

I'll use my husband and myself as an example. This year we chose to state our first goal in this way: "Our number-one goal is to have a closer walk with God." Now you may want to break that down and detail it. You might decide to enhance your walk with God by reading ten chapters of the Bible each day or by spending an hour a day praying in the Holy Spirit. There are lots of ways to have a closer walk with God. Whatever your strategy, you are positioning yourself to hear the voice of God more clearly, to experience His presence, and to know His perfect will for your life. The number-one goal each year for Mel and me is to get closer to God. Our scriptural verse for this is Matthew 6:33: "But seek first the kingdom of God and His righteousness, and all these things shall be added to you." What things? In this case, they are the rest of your goals!

First and foremost, be sure your priorities are in order. There's success, and then there's good success. A lot of people are successful in some areas, but they're also strung out on drugs. They're miserable. They hate their lives. The way to enjoy the whole journey is to keep Christ at the center of your motives, your heart, and everything about who you are. God can take the simplest person in the world, and if that person will dare to believe what's written in His Word, He will empower him/her to accomplish anything godly he/she desires.

7. Stay on course.

The final step in goal-setting is to stay on course. Maybe you have a long way to go in attaining your ideal weight. Set your goals and stick with them. Don't grow weary while doing well.

And let us not grow weary while doing good, for in due season we shall reap if we do not lose heart.

—GALATIANS 6:9

It all comes back to the condition of your heart. It's usually when you think you're doing well that the enemy will try to drag you into something so overwhelming that you'll begin to feel sorry for yourself. You grow weary in your heart and you lose focus of your goals. Let me encourage you here: protect your heart. Why is this so critical? Because if you don't lose heart, you'll reap a great reward!

At the beginning of every new year, Mel and I review our previous year's goals and share our new ones. Then we pray over them. I encourage you to do this with someone close to you and celebrate one another's victories. Also, be sure to encourage one another if you did not reach last year's goals. Consider rolling them over into the New Year!

8. Choose to focus on the positive.

Good things and bad things are happening all the time. Choose to focus on the positive things that are happening. Choose life. Choose to set your sights and your heart on what is good. In Philippians 4:8 we are told to set our minds on or meditate on whatever things are true, noble, just, pure, lovely, and of a good report. It doesn't say to think on whatever things are bad, ugly, negative, terrible, and hurtful. We need to be discerning; to guard our hearts and ask God for wisdom in every situation. Every great work, every big accomplishment has been brought into manifestation through holding to the vision.

If you are feeling weary, encourage yourself, for your breakthrough may be just around the corner. Over and over Mel and I have found that the biggest hit, discouragement, or apparent failure comes just before the biggest breakthrough. History has demonstrated that the most notable winners usually encountered heartbreaking obstacles just before they triumphed. They won because they refused to become discouraged. Thomas Edison said, "I have not failed. I just found 10,000 ways that won't work!" I like that attitude. In other words, he tried many ways that didn't work but gained a lot of wisdom through the process!

Follow the steps in this chapter and allow God to help you accomplish the goals and visions He has specifically for you.

Goals

Vision

4

TWO TOOLS FOR ACHIEVING YOUR DESIRED WEIGHT

〜

N OW WE WILL turn our attention to two major tools to victory over addictions, eating disorders, and anything that comes between you and God and the wonderful life He has planned for you. These tools are the *Word of God* and *prayer*; the very tools that empowered me to go from feeling and looking chubby, plump, and overweight to feeling and looking like a victorious woman of God with self-control over her body. I believe these spiritual weapons will work for whoever will take hold of them and use them. You are destined to win this battle. Get ready to take hold of these spiritual weapons, win the spiritual battle, and watch the victory manifest in your natural body weight!

THE WORD OF GOD

The Bible tells us that we overcome "by the blood of the Lamb and the word of [our] testimony" (Rev. 12:11). Isn't that great news? Our victory is not dependent on our circumstances or our feelings, both of which are subject to change and must line up with the Word of God. Instead, our victory is based on what Christ has done for us and by the word of our own testimony.

> In the beginning was the Word, and the Word was with God, and the Word was God.
>
> —JOHN 1:1

This verse tells us that when we're talking about the Word of God, we're talking about God Himself. God and His Word are one. Often when people are in trouble, they say that they wish God would walk into the room and talk to them. In fact, all we have to do is open up the Bible and He'll speak to us. I love the acronym B-I-B-L-E, which stands for Basic Instructions Before Leaving Earth! This means that we can turn to God, to His Word, for the answer to any problem we have.

John 8:32 tell us: "You shall know the truth, and the truth shall make you free." This says that knowing the truth, which is the Word, will set us free. As we live on earth, the enemy will try to show up to oppress or depress us. Or perhaps there are situations in our lives or feelings we are carrying that we desperately want to be free of! Here we see that we can get to that place of freedom, security, strength, health, and peace by knowing the truth; by knowing the Word of God. But, we have to go after the truth. We have to pick up the Bible and use it as a weapon.

In Ephesians 6:17, the Word of God is described as a sword. It reads: "The sword of the Spirit, which is the word of God." It's also the only spiritual weapon of offense that we're given. Sometimes as children of God we're saved, we love God, and we walk in righteousness as best we can. However, it's almost as if we're standing around getting beaten up by the enemy of our souls with all the trials and challenges that come our way. It's not until we take the Word of God and speak it out that we're fighting in the spirit realm. We're fighting with our sword of the Spirit, and we're actually cleansing the entire atmosphere. In fact, we have even been given authority over devils. (See Luke 9:1.)

God gave me a vision a while ago when I was praying. In the spirit realm, He showed me a battlefield with landmines, cannons, flying bullets, and many kinds of war activity. He also showed me Christians walking around barefooted. They were in a tremendous war, they had on no armor, and their swords were on the ground. Therefore, they were easy targets; wide open to getting wounded or becoming casualties of the spiritual battle that was going on all around them. Christians are in a war whether they know it or not. Our powerful offensive weapon is the sword of the Spirit, which is the Word of God. However, we must pick up that weapon, speak the Word of God, and declare victory in the battles we are facing.

Let me give you an example of one area the enemy uses to come at us to try and get us all bound up within ourselves. Remember, he purposes to keep us from obtaining wisdom, speaking truth and life over ourselves, and obtaining the victories we so desire. Do you ever find yourself having a little pity party? It's not something you plan to do, you just get under pressure—and under your circumstances—and all of a sudden it's "poor me" time and you're seeing yourself as a victim.

Recently I was in our swimming pool by myself and I had been praying. There were a few difficult things going on in my life at the time and I needed to hear from heaven. But the more I thought, the more I started to get tangled up in my emotions. I began to feel overwhelmed and feel sorry for myself, and then I started to cry. Thankfully, in this case, I caught myself looking back on situations and realized I was really dealing with grief.

The key to my getting victory that day was that I knew the Word of God says I have authority in the spirit realm. So I said, "Grief, you go in Jesus' name!" Immediately, grief left. In that situation, I made the choice to go by God's Word rather than be bound by my emotions.

Now, there's nothing necessarily wrong with emotions, but we can't allow them to rule our lives. Rather, we need to be ruled by God's Word. You, too, can take authority in the realm of your emotions. Remember, emotions affect how we perceive things, which, in turn, affect the decisions we make, including those related to our health, our weight, and our self-esteem.

I'm grateful that I came to this realization quickly that day. Sometimes, however, we let ourselves stay in that funk for hours, even days, wrestling to pull ourselves out. It's better to nip it in the beginning. Discern what you're feeling and deal with it or rebuke it in Jesus' name. Speak God's Word over the situation out loud to yourself and over yourself, and watch that funk lift and the issues get resolved.

Oppression, depression, and the heaviness you may be feeling are products of the spirit realm. They are demonic and do not belong on you or near you, and the only reason you allow it at all is because it is a "familiar" spirit. Your mama probably had it, your papa probably had it, your grandma may have had it, and it just gets passed along. You've just become used to it, so you let it into your life. You're so comfortable with it that it almost seems like a friend. Oppressive, negative emotions and "drama" are not your friends. They will hurt you in your soul, your mind, your will, your emotions, and your body. Remember, we have a tool, a weapon, in the Word of God to totally rid ourselves of them. Hebrews 4:12 says:

> For the Word of God is living and powerful, and sharper than any two-edged sword, piercing even to the division of soul and spirit, and of joints and marrow, and is a discerner of the thoughts and intents of the heart.

Let's focus on the fact that the Word is active and powerful. That's the reason it's your answer to everything, no matter what you're going through. That's why at different seasons of your life the same scripture can minister to your heart in different ways.

In terms of pressing in to get free of an addiction, illnesses, or eating disorder, consider this assignment. This transformed my life and I know it will do the same for you. Read your Bible from Matthew to Revelation with the idea that "this is the area where I want freedom." If you're battling a weight problem and it seems like you can't get free of it no matter how long or how many times you've tried, or no matter what diet you've been on, understand that the root is a spiritual issue. The root needs to be addressed from this standpoint. As you read through the entire New Testament, underline everything that stands out as being significant to the area where you need freedom. Copy the scriptures you've underlined into a notebook or journal so that you have them available to read and confess any time you feel like you want to binge, purge, drink, smoke, or indulge in anything not good for you. Any time you are tempted in any way, take out your list of scriptures and start confessing the Word instead of dwelling on the temptation or following its path. It will set you free every time!

What you're saying about yourself is so important. Are you looking in the mirror and saying, "I'm so fat!"? Don't do that. The Word of God says, "Death and life are in the power of your tongue" (Prov. 18:21). You are declaring who and what you are when you speak about yourself. Your tongue is a rudder that can change the entire course of your life. Instead, look into the mirror and say, "Thank You, God, that I'm the righteousness of God in Christ Jesus. I am fit and in shape. In the name of Jesus, I walk or work out several times a week." Speak life and freedom over yourself. Be sure to declare it out loud and act on the Word.

I remember when I was first getting ahold of this revelation many years ago. I was going on acting auditions and if I did not get picked, I was not a happy camper. Like most people, I do not like rejection. Trying to get work in Hollywood is definitely not the field for sensitive people who struggle with rejection.

I remember one particular audition. Without anyone saying a word, I could tell I didn't get the part. Here I had driven all the way to Hollywood, and I had waited and worked my way through all these people, but I knew I wasn't going to get called for the job. I started to feel upset and then I thought, "I think I'll go to Mrs. Fields cookies and eat about six cookies to make myself feel better."

At the same time I could feel the Holy Spirit telling me, "That's not right." So I said "Okay, God. Then this is what I'm going to do. I'm going to go home and read your Word for five to ten minutes, and if after that I don't feel better, I'm going to go out and get Mrs. Fields cookies." I just talked straightforwardly with God. I was honest with Him, but I was also obedient to go home and read His Word. As I read and reviewed my own personal journal of scriptures (like the one I mentioned above), immediately the power of God hit me and I felt great. I had myself a banana and said, "God, this works! It works! It really works! The Word of God is real. It's alive! It's quick and powerful! It's more powerful than Mrs. Fields cookies!"

There certainly is power in His Word. Psalm 107:20 says, "He sent His word and healed them, And delivered them from their destructions." The Word is Jesus. Jesus will heal you. The Bible says that God sent his Word and healed them. That's you and that's me! You may have heard this scripture a thousand times. Well, it's good to hear it again. As you continue to hear the Word of God, it will bring you health and healing.

As the Word of God is preached, your faith is built up. Romans 10:17 tells us: "So then faith comes by hearing, and hearing by the word of God." Sometimes you'll see brand-new Christians operate in faith and get tremendous miracles. Why? Because they're spiritually hungry and they saturate themselves in the Word of God. Whether you've been a Christian for one year or twenty, miracles happen when you're saturated in the Word of God. When the Word of God is what you're hearing, meditating on, and speaking out, you're setting yourself up to see miracles. Your faith is built up. Why? Because you're in the Word of God. To those who will believe what God says, all things are possible!

It's also important to spend time with people who talk the Word of God rather than nonsense. If you spend much time with people who are not talking the Word of God, it can bring your faith level down. It's true that we're called to minister to people, but whoever is doing the talking is doing the ministering. That's why you need to ask God for discernment about people. Are they understanding and receiving what you're sharing? Then, when you tell them something, do they do it? That's how you know whom to minister to and whom to spend time with. In all the give and take of relationships, the Word of God needs to be in first place in your life, and you need to be around others who also receive it and put it first in their lives!

I heard a story from Pastor Casey Treat at a ministry conference.1 He said, "It's very hard sometimes as a spiritual leader, because there are so many needs and there are so many people, and you're put in that situation where you need to make very difficult choices."[1] He compared it to a scene in the movie *Pearl Harbor*. In this scene, a nurse walked outside and had to pick which of the wounded she would allow into the hospital and which ones she wouldn't. There were thousands of people coming; most were burned and severely injured, but there were only a few nurses. There was no way they could save all the wounded people. She had to choose who would live and who would die.

It's really not so different for any of us who are believers. We're out there in the world and we have to have wisdom as we pick and choose how and with whom we spend our time, especially concerning where we're investing our time to help people. We have to discern who has ears to hear. Who's really going to grow? Who's going to grab on to what we believe and affect the multitudes? There will be those who do nothing, complain, and fail to grow up in the Lord. We need to choose wisely which lives we will invest in. These can be hard and sometimes unpopular decisions; but we must make the tough calls.

Psalm 119:105 says, "Your word is a lamp to my feet." God, by His Word, will guide you in your life. He'll use His Word to guide you, but you have to be reading it. When you are, suddenly you'll get a flash of insight into something and say, "Yes, that's what I need to do. Thank You, Jesus, for speaking to me about that subject." God's Word is alive; it's quick and it's powerful!

In addition, the Word will make you successful. Joshua 1:8 tells us:

> This Book of the Law shall not depart from your mouth, but you shall meditate in it day and night, that you may observe to do according to all that is written in it. For then you will make your way prosperous, and then you will have good success.

Reading the Word will give you wisdom for making the best decisions. Decisions will help you prosper and succeed in every area of your life, whether in relationships, work, finances, or in your health and appearance. The Word is seed that will sustain you. It's spiritual seed to feed you. Some people are starving spiritually. They just need to dine on the Word of God. Matthew 4:4 says:

> It is written, "Man shall not live by bread alone, but by every word that proceeds from the mouth of God."

His Word fills us on the inside. Cookie dough will not, nor will bread. What really fills us is the Word of God. Not only is the Word nourishing food, but it's also sustaining water. Jesus is "rivers of living water" flowing through you (John 7:38).

> But whoever drinks of the water that I shall give him will never thirst. But the water that I shall give him

will become in him a fountain of water springing up
into everlasting life.

—JOHN 4:14

His living water is something we can receive every day
and at any time. When you find yourself waist high in His
living water, I encourage you to say, "That's not enough. I'm
going deeper and getting *filled* with rivers of living water!"
Another scripture relevant to this is Romans 13:14:

> But clothe yourself with the Lord Jesus Christ (the
> Messiah), and make no provision for [indulging] the
> flesh [put a stop to thinking about the evil cravings of
> your physical nature] to [gratify its] desires (lusts).
>
> —AMP

Now that's a powerful word. It's telling you to stop thinking about the mound of chocolate you want to pound down,
or whatever area it is that you want to "flesh-out" in, stop it.
It says to instead clothe yourself with the Lord Jesus Christ.
In other words, meditate on the Word day and night!

PRAYER, OUR SECOND TOOL

Your second supernatural tool is prayer. Anything I have
ever seen manifest in my life that's been positive, lovely, and
of a good report, I've seen in prayer first. I have prayed for
those things and have seen them manifest. I've also found
that one hour of prayer a day will keep the temptation away.
And let's face it; food is a tremendous temptation for most
people. Matthew 26:41 says:

> Watch and pray, lest you enter into temptation. The
> spirit indeed is willing, but the flesh is weak.

In this portion of Matthew, Jesus tells Peter he will deny Him. Peter told Jesus, "There's no way I will deny You! I will not deny You!" And Jesus told Peter, "Yes, you will." Peter then said, "Even if I have to die, I will not deny You. I will not!" (See Matthew 26:31–35.) I really believe that at that moment Jesus knew what was going to happen, but His heart went out to Peter because He saw Peter's earnest desire to do the right thing. Okay Peter, you want to do the right thing? Then *"watch and pray lest you enter into temptation."* The temptation was of denying the living God, the Christ whom Peter had seen raise the dead and perform miracle after miracle.

Jesus knew that Peter was about to be put in a life or death situation and would deny Him, so He said, "The spirit indeed is willing, but the flesh is weak" (Matt. 26:41). Peter's spirit man was saying, "Yes, I want to stand behind you." However, when push came to shove, Peter's flesh gave in. Let's read what happened next:

> Again, a second time, He [Jesus] went away and prayed, saying, "O My Father, if this cup cannot pass away from Me unless I drink it, Your will be done." And He came and found them asleep again, for their eyes were heavy. So He left them, went away again, and prayed the third time, saying the same words. Then He came to His disciples and said to them, "Are you still sleeping and resting?"
> —MATTHEW 26:42–45

Even though Jesus had asked His disciples to stay awake and pray, they did not. In fact, He asked them to pray one hour. I think that's a key for all of us—one hour. I believe that in the scripture God is saying that with one hour in prayer you will be able to beat the temptation. Perhaps one hour was all it would have taken for Peter to not have denied the Christ, the Son of the living God. But, he didn't pray. Instead, he fell asleep.

How many times has God called you to pray, but you've fallen asleep? Do you ever find yourself waking up at 4:00 or 5:00 in the morning? Do you know why? It's not so you can take a Tylenol PM. I believe it means you're supposed to pray. At that moment, God is looking for an intercessor to pray. He's looking for whoever will pray. All you have to do is just get up and pray! God needs you to pray. There is something crucial going on in the spirit realm and He's looking for somebody to pray. We may be living in an earth suit, our earthly body, but we are living in a spirit realm as well.

What is prayer? It's simply talking to God.

> Tragedy is un-prayed prayer, not unanswered prayer.[2]
> —RUTH GRAHAM

> Whether your goal is to witness to one man or preach the gospel to the nation, you will succeed or fail based entirely on your prayer life.[3]
> —KENNETH COPELAND

> God will do nothing but in answer to prayer.[4]
> —JOHN WESLEY

The leaders of the Clapham Sect of British social reformers such as William Wilberforce, daily gave themselves to three hours of prayer and organized Christians throughout the country to unite in special prayers before critical debates in Parliament. William Temple replied to his critics who regarded answered prayer as no more than coincidence, "When I pray, coincidences happen; when I don't, they don't."[5]

Prayer gives you strength to fulfill the God-given purpose of your life. It's like a divine infusion.

- 🌷 Prayer is preparation for something great in your life to take place.

- 🌷 Prayer produces the overcomer.

- 🌷 All spiritual victories are won in prayer.

One of the last points I want to share with you on prayer is regarding praying in other tongues, or praying in the Spirit. What a gift of God praying in the Spirit is! Do you want power? Do you want the supernatural power of God working in your life?

> But you shall receive power when the Holy Spirit has come upon you; and you shall be witnesses to Me in Jerusalem, and in all Judea and Samaria, and to the end of the earth.
>
> —Acts 1:8

What a wonderful promise. Now let's look at Romans 8:26:

> Likewise the Spirit also helps in our weaknesses. For we do not know what we should pray for as we ought, but the Spirit Himself makes intercession for us with groanings which cannot be uttered.

Many times when we're praying for people or loved ones we assume that we know what's going on, but we may not know the core issue that is holding them in a devastating situation. Sometimes the same thing holds true for our own issues and situations. Sometimes we need the Holy Spirit to help us with our own "blind spots."

Romans 8:26 tells us that if we pray in other tongues, we're praying the perfect prayer. I don't know everything, nor do you, but the Holy Spirit does. By praying in the Spirit, we open our hearts and lives in a way that allows us to intercede on behalf of others. We can lift them to the Lord and pray for exactly what they need.

Jude 1:20 is a scripture that is key to this topic and a good one to turn to when you're feeling down. When you're not flying from mountaintop to mountaintop or glory to glory, read this verse:

> But you, beloved, build yourselves up [founded] on your most holy faith [make progress, rise like an edifice higher and higher], praying in the Holy Spirit.
>
> —AMP

As we pray in the Holy Spirit, we literally build up the person inside us. It's a powerhouse gift, but we need to choose to do it. If you want peace, health, strength, and life, then pray in the Spirit and declare the Word. I recommend doing this in the morning before you begin your day. Place yourself in an atmosphere where God can speak to you and you can listen. And remember, the Word does not return to Him void. (See Isaiah 55:10–11.)

Another benefit of praying in the Spirit is that it delivers us from our flesh, where eating disorders reside.

> I say then: Walk in the Spirit, and you shall not fulfill the lust of the flesh. For the flesh lusts against the Spirit, and the Spirit against the flesh; and these are contrary to one another, so you do not do the things that you wish.
>
> —GALATIANS 5:16–17

A classic example of this is food. Have you ever made a decision to eat raw vegetables or lean protein or just to eat healthy? You're determined. You're on your new program of working out and eating correctly. But then all of a sudden it's 3:00 in the afternoon and you see those "golden arches." Just a quick little drive-through, and before you know it you're eating French fries while you're driving home or on to your next errand. Has something like that ever happened to you? Your spirit really wanted to eat those raw carrots and celery. That was the plan. But then those French fries, oh so soft, crunchy, and salty! Your flesh got the better of you. It's a battle, but daily we need to ask ourselves, "Am I going to live today by the flesh or by the Spirit?

As I've pointed out earlier, before I married my husband, I was a stuntwoman and I was anorexic and bulimic. Nobody knew it though. I looked fine on the outside, but on the inside I was not a healthy person. I was using diuretics and laxatives, and doing all kinds of crazy things to look the way I thought I needed to look in order to get work. But inside I felt like I was dying. In fact, I knew I was dying. My hair was falling out and my nails were falling off. I finally confessed to my husband what was going on. Together, we prayed a prayer of agreement, we stood on the Word of God for my healing, *and* we prayed in the Spirit.

Please note a few of the keys here. The first is *agreement*. The second is *stand on the Word of God*. And the third is *pray in the Spirit*. I found out that if I prayed in the Holy Spirit when I felt like I just wanted to go eat and then vomit, any craving I had for cookie dough or anything else that was unhealthy immediately left me. I could eat a banana instead and be satisfied, really satisfied.

Now, this wasn't some sort of mind control I was using,

nor was it a diet. There was something else involved with this whole issue of food for me. In some instances it was a straight flesh/self-control problem. Other times it was spiritual warfare and a brazen attack of the enemy to oppress or deceive my mind, so I'd be more prone to stumble and eat unhealthy food.

I remember one time when I was on the verge of a binge. I went to the grocery store and bought all of the ingredients to make chocolate chip cookie dough. Most people who have a problem with binging know that by the time you buy everything you want to eat and are on the way home to eat you are history. You would have to catch yourself before you bought all the junk to keep from eating it. As I was stirring all of the ingredients together, I decided to give this praying in the spirit thing a try. As I began to pray in tongues the power of God filled me, and I fell on my knees (in this tiny kitchen, with a giant bowl of cookie dough) and began to praise and worship God for His awesome presence and power. I stood up after several minutes and threw the cookie dough down the drain without even taking an itty-bitty bite! That was a miracle! Those of you who struggle with binge eating know what I am talking about. I discovered a powerful tool on my road to complete victory.

Whatever the situation, I discovered that by praying in the Holy Spirit I was building myself up, making myself strong, and placing myself in a position to say no to that which I shouldn't be doing. As surely as it worked for me, it will work for you. I love that God is not a respecter of persons and His spiritual principles are for anyone who will use them.

In Matthew 18:19–20, we learn about the power of agreement in prayer:

Again I say to you that if two of you agree on earth

concerning anything that they ask, it will be done for them by My Father in heaven. For where two or three are gathered together in My name, I am there in the midst of them.

That should build up your faith. God keeps His Word. He hears and answers us when we call on Him, believe Him, and come into agreement concerning whatever we ask of Him. I want to come into agreement with you right now regarding your situation and regarding your healing, your restoration, and victory as it pertains to your being free from addictions or eating disorders.

The following is an Overcomer's Confession that I've used in the process of my own healing. It is a confession that resulted in changing my feelings and gaining victory over my food problem. When we are in agreement with and say what God says, it's done! As you read and speak out the following, believe that it's true in your situation and know that I am standing in agreement with you for your victory:

> *Father, lead me not into temptation today or any day, but deliver me from evil. I will not let the devil take advantage of me and sift me as wheat. I trust in You alone to provide an escape from all temptation.*
>
> *My strength comes from the power of the Lord as I clothe myself with the whole armor of God...*
>
> *The belt of truth I will use to bind my innermost parts with Your truth.*
>
> *The breastplate of righteousness will protect my heart, for out of it flow the issues of life.*
>
> *The shoes of the readiness of the gospel of peace give me the stability to proclaim the gospel that Jesus died, was buried, and rose again to those in my path today.*
>
> *The shield of faith I will lift up; it does not keep me*

from the battle, but protects me in the midst of it!

The helmet of salvation I wear to shelter my mind from Satan's attacks of doubt, depression, and discouragement.

The sword of the Spirit is the Word of God, which I use to defeat the devil.

I will praise You! I will put on a garment of praise in exchange for the spirit of heaviness.

I am more than a conqueror through the blood of Jesus. I am redeemed out of the hand of Satan. I am cleansed continually from all sin. I am justified and made holy and set apart to God. I am free from the fear of hell and death. I am healed of all sickness, disease, and guilt. I am forgiven and all my sins are forgotten. I choose to forget them too. I know Satan is a bluff, a liar, and a thief. Satan has no place, no power, and no unsettled claims against me. On the Cross the battle was won. Satan was made a public display. I have authority over all the powers of darkness. I fear nothing!

I have the same power in me that raised Jesus from the dead. Jesus and His power are the same yesterday, today, and forever. I can do all things through Christ Jesus who strengthens me. I'm an overcomer by the blood of the Lamb and the word of my testimony, and I love not my life unto death.

Father, I ask that every carnal prayer, every negative statement, and every curse spoken against me or by me be broken in the name of Jesus. I ask that the harvest of negative seeds I have sown be cut short, and the harvest of positive seeds be hastened, for I know that as I have sown, I will reap. Fill me with the knowledge of your will today and of all spiritual wisdom and understanding, so that I may walk in a manner worthy of You, to please You, bearing good fruit and increasing in the knowledge of You. Amen!

5

PUT OFF EXTRA WEIGHTS

W HAT DO LOVE and forgiveness have to do with eating disorders or getting free of strongholds and addictions? A lot! This may sound strange, but some people have problems with constipation simply because they have unforgivingness in their hearts. They are all stopped up, so to speak, in their emotions and their condition is manifesting in their bodies. They need to forgive others, let go of past hurts and misunderstandings, and may even need to forgive themselves. When they do this, their bodies will do likewise. You may laugh at this, but in ministry I've found it to be true. We are a spirit, a soul, and a body, and what happens in our spirit and in our soul affects our physical body.

God wired us with emotions, but He did not intend for us to be ruled by them. Yet many people are emotional eaters. They get into situations where they're offended and then they struggle with what follows: hurt, pain, anger, resentment, unforgivingness, fatigue, or sickness. Rather than run to the presence of God—where there is comfort, forgiveness, order, healing, peace, and strength—they live in and operate from their emotions. Their emotions can go haywire on them, drawing them back into the offense and into its harmful effects. Rather than turn to and fill up on God, they fill up on food. The answer, of course, is to run to God and fill up on His love and comfort!

Unforgivingness can be a learned behavior or it can be part of a generational pattern or curse. One side of my own family is very unforgiving. They get their feelings hurt, they get offended easily, and they hold on to grudges. Unfortunately, there's also a generational curse of cancer on that side of the family. You need to understand that there is a connection between your spirit, soul, and body.

The bottom line is that even if there is unforgivingness throughout our family, we have the Word of God that teaches us how to forgive. We can break free of strongholds by turning to Jesus and receiving His Word as final authority in every area of our lives and with every emotion. John 8:36 says, "If the Son makes you free, you shall be free indeed."

I have spent a lot of time studying the subject of forgiveness because I've found it to be an area of weakness in my own life. I've also discovered that if you'll apply the Word of God in that area, what was once a weakness designed by the enemy to take you out can become your strength. Remember, God's Word is alive and transforming. It can turn your life around.

God's Word Brings Life and Healing

We'll now focus on key scriptures about healing, love, and forgiveness. I will share some of my own personal stories and how I applied the Word to be set free. I encourage you to receive God's Word in your spirit because it brings life and healing. It can set you free, just as it did me!

Jesus had many things to say about choosing to receive and to give love and forgiveness. First of all, He reminds us that we are to love God and love one another. Jesus says:

> And you shall love the Lord your God with all your heart, with all your soul, with all your mind, and with all your strength. This is the first commandment. And the second, like it, is this: "You shall love your neighbor as yourself." There is no other commandment greater than these.
>
> —MARK 12:30–31

Often I find that it's easy to love God. It's the other people He created that can be difficult to love at times. However, God would never ask us to do something that we are incapable of doing; so know this, you can love others.

Next, we must recognize that forgiving and being willing to forgive are the right things to do. One of my earliest experiences with learning to forgive happened just a few months into my marriage. I shared with my husband, Mel, about my past relationship with an alcoholic boyfriend who had physically abused me. The response I received from Mel shocked me. He told me that I needed to forgive my ex-boyfriend. I thought, *Forgive him? You must be kidding!* I had told Mel this story so he would side with me and want to beat this guy up. I had imagined Mel and I taking him on, kicking and stomping on him until he was bruised and bleeding!

I didn't particularly like Mel's answer. But in my newly born-again spirit, I understood that my husband was right. I was going to have to forgive my ex-boyfriend. Still stunned by Mel's answer, I simply said, "Okay." Then I decided to go to the beach for a run to try to process this new concept—forgiving what I believed to be the unforgivable.

Mel and I lived in Manhattan Beach, California, and I loved to run along the ocean. As I headed towards the majestic sea in the beautiful late afternoon sunshine, I acknowledged the truth that I needed to forgive and asked God to help me to do that.

Within a few minutes of that prayer, believe it or not, I ran in to my ex-boyfriend, the one who had hurt and tried to kill me. Now, I had not seen this guy or talked to him in years. (Sounds like a God set-up, doesn't it?) I approached him and asked if we could talk, which we did for several minutes. Then I looked at him and told him that I forgave him for all he had done to me. As I did this, I felt a release. He, on the other hand, went white as a ghost and didn't know what to say. That day I experienced my first encounter with the principle that the one who forgives is the one who is set free.

A few years after that encounter, Mel and I ran into him again and had the awesome opportunity and joy of leading my ex-boyfriend to the Lord. God can truly turn any situation around for His glory and our benefit. Trust Him. Believe that He will, for freedom is available to you this very day.

After this experience I thought that I had the concept of forgiveness down, but I still had much to learn. A few years later I found myself in a situation where I wanted to forgive a certain someone, but I just couldn't. Have you ever felt like that?

Back in the 1980s, when I was working as a stuntwoman in Hollywood, I experienced firsthand the difficulty of obeying the scripture to love one of God's children. I also experienced freedom once I chose to obey. I believe the revelation I am going to show you will set you free forever as you apply these easy Biblical steps Jesus so clearly walks us through.

In 1985, while working on a television set, I was literally blown up. My face, neck, and arms received second- and third-degree burns during one of the stunts I was working on. Ten days later I walked out of the burn center with a miraculous healing, which is chronicled in my book, *Beyond the Flame.*[1]

What really hurt my heart throughout this whole affair, however, were the actions of a girlfriend who was becoming very successful in her work after my having helped her get her start in the stunt business. During my time of healing and transition of careers, I expected her to continue to be my friend. I found out, however, that she was only interested in being my friend when I was a working stuntwoman who could help her get jobs. In fact, I found that many people were not interested in having a relationship with me after I was no longer in a position to help them. The one person who hurt me the most, however, was this close friend who severed our relationship during the time when I felt down and out. Thoughts went through my mind like: *Real friends are supposed to stick with you through the tough times. I helped her when she was down and out! Where is she now that I'm struggling and my heart is bleeding?* Of course, those thoughts only got me deeper into the realm of bitterness and unforgivingness, which, in turn, blocked my heart from love.

Mel and I were walking on the beach one day when I turned to him for help and support. I had chosen to talk to him about this issue because I wanted to be set free. We can go to different people for different things, but certain people will give us the truth. Mel is that person for me. He gives me the truth even though, at times, it hurts. Often he'll say, "Desiree, it's you," which he did in this instance. My response was, "What about this betrayal? What about my feelings?" He just said, "Desiree, you've got to get free. This is a stronghold in your life. You've got to forgive her."

I finally agreed, and then we prayed for her. I felt so much better for a couple of weeks, but slowly I began to feel my heart becoming hard towards her again. I continued to cry out to God for help and He gave me a scripture that strengthened me to win this battle. I can't wait to share it with you because it has the power to set you free. It's Luke 6:27–28, and here's what it says:

> But I say to you who hear: Love your enemies, do good to those who hate you, bless those who curse you, and pray for those who spitefully use you.

STEPS TO FORGIVENESS

There are three simple steps to this scripture that will turn you back into the love-vessel you were created to be.

The first step is to pray. Pray for the person who has offended you. The moment I started to pray for my friend, my heart began to soften. Here's what happened. Through my prayers God gave me tiny glimpses into her childhood and what her life was like back then. I saw that she never had examples of unconditional love from parents who were full of Christ. She had only been saved for the two years that I was in her life. After leading her to the Lord, I had begun to take her to church with me. Overall, she had a lot of trust issues. She finally had a chance to make it some-where and was trying to protect that. As God showed me this, He began filling me with His own compassion; my heart softened, and I began to truly care for her. God does minister to people as we pray for them, but we are set free in the meantime.

The second step is to bless. Bless means to speak well of someone. I became free that day on the beach when I prayed with Mel. I was set free at that instant, but later I picked up that burden again and got caught in the chains of entrapment. This happened when someone mentioned this girl's name in a negative way and I chimed in, "Oh yeah, she's just a climber; she'll step on anyone to get to the top." After those words came out of my mouth, I felt bitterness start to set in again. I was not blessing her. I was cutting her down. I realized I needed to change and made a decision that the words that came out of my mouth would only bless her. I determined that regardless of what anyone else said about her or how hard it might be, I would find something kind to say about her. As I applied this truth about blessing, I became completely free and full of love again.

> Therefore let us pursue the things which make for peace and the things by which one may edify another.
> —ROMANS 14:19

> Let each one of us please his neighbor for his good, leading to [his or her] edification.
> —ROMANS 15:2

Step three is to do "good." You may want to give the person a gift or do something that will just bless their socks off. When you do, you'll experience the joy and freedom God has for you.

> Bearing with one another, and forgiving one another,
> if anyone has a complaint against another; even as
> Christ forgave you, so you also must do. But above
> all these things put on love, which is the bond of
> perfection.
>
> —COLOSSIANS 3:13–14

Here's how wonderful the Lord is. Eventually, healing came into my relationship with her. Now there are no hard feelings whatsoever. Instead, we have the love of Christ in our hearts for one another. However, it took that scripture in Luke to change my life forever, and since then, I have applied it over and over and over again!

The choice to forgive, to pray, to bless, and to do "good" is huge with the Lord. I pray that if this is an area of struggle for you, it will instead develop into an area of strength for you. You are created to be a vessel of love for God. Simply decide that you are that vessel and then begin to act like it.

It's important for us to understand that if we are the ones that are offended; we are the ones with the problem. This is a shocking thought to most of us because it's so easy to believe that it's always the other person's fault.

The Lord shows us how we are to handle hurtful or offensive situations. Most importantly, He compels us to keep our hearts right with Him, to keep our hearts yielded to Him, and to trust Him during every moment of the process.

Here's what the Bible says about this:

> Judge not, that you be not judged. For with what judgment you judge, you will be judged; and with the measure you use, it will be measured back to you. And why do you look at the speck in your brother's eye, but

do not consider the plank in your own eye? Or how can you say to your brother, 'Let me remove the speck from your eye'; and look, a plank is in your own eye? Hypocrite! First remove the plank from your own eye, and then you will see clearly to remove the speck from your brother's eye.

—MATTHEW 7:1–2

Being easily offended, holding grudges, and having hurt feelings are like planks in our own eyes. We must get rid of them in order to see clearly and to live in freedom. The spirit of being easily offended and unable to forgive is not from God. It's from hell, and we must refuse it and cast it out of our lives.

The Bible teaches that when you cast something demonic (such as unforgivingness or an addiction) out of a house (the "house" refers to your life), you empty the house. Once it is empty, however, you must refill your life with God and His Word. If you don't, what you cast out will return, but not just by itself. According to Scripture, it will return with reinforcements, with seven more demons. (See Matthew 12:45.)

It's so important that your house (your life) be full of the Word of God so that those demons won't even want to come near you. Nothing and no one can successfully come up against God and His Word! When you're saturated in the Word, those demons are afraid you're going to quote the scripture that sent them flying the last time. They don't want to hear it and they'll go somewhere else.

I had to recognize that I needed to get scriptures on love and forgiveness into my heart and meditate on them. When I did this, I was empowered to live in victory, freedom, and peace.

A CHOICE TO LIVE OUT GOD'S WORD

This next battle drove me to a deeper place of understanding the importance of keeping the Word in my heart and in my mouth, and of choosing to live out the Word of God in my life. A few years after my major victory over taking offense, I found that spirit trying to creep back into my life. It happened at a time when I had tremendous back pain. For months I couldn't sleep at night. I would be fine for a few days after being prayed for in a healing service, but then the pain would return. In prayer I asked God, "What in the world is going on? I've experienced your healing miracles many times and I minister healing to others. I just don't understand what's happening."

God in His loving way spoke back to me, "Desiree, you are hurting so much on the inside, it's manifesting itself on the outside." I cried and agreed with the Lord. "Yes, Lord, I know that's it." As many tears rolled down my cheeks, I wallowed in self-pity. What He said next, however, shocked me to my very core. He said, "Desiree, you are hurting because you are not forgiving. When you forgive, you will no longer hurt!"

This was hard for me to hear. Now I had to accept that I was no longer the victim, but actually the cause of my problem. I could no longer blame my problem on others. I was wrong, not the people that I wanted to blame for causing my hurt. It was no longer their fault; it was mine. Ouch!

Once again I had been the disobedient child. Now in response to this revelation, I cried, acknowledged my sin, repented, and asked the Lord to help me change. I went back to Luke 6 and focused on doing "good." I bought presents for and served the people that I felt were taking advantage of me, the very ones I felt were being selfish and cruel towards my husband and me.

The truth, however, is that we can't change other people. We can only work on changing ourselves and must leave the changing of other people in God's hands. In the area of marriage, many husbands and wives would do well to learn to love, pray, do good, and bless their spouses... and stop trying to change them.

My husband and I figured this out when we first got married. In the beginning of our marriage, we would really get into it. I think I'm pretty sweet now (at least, I think so), but I wasn't then. I was feisty and I liked to fight and throw things. I used to wear high heels, so when I'd get mad at Mel, I'd take off my shoe and go right for his head. Mel would have to duck to miss the blow.

Mel would go into his prayer room during those times and pray, because not only was his wife physically out of control, but she was emotionally out of control as well. Even though I had been crying, throwing things, and saying all kinds of garbage, when Mel would pray about our argument the Lord would tell him to apologize to me. Now, who do you think was really in the wrong most of the time? Sometimes it was fifty-fifty, but most of the time I was the one who had been wrong. Still, God would tell Mel to apologize to me for allowing strife into our home. So, he'd come from his time of prayer and tell me that he was sorry. In response, I'd say something like, "It's about time you apologized to me!" Of course, that would make Mel angry again and we'd start arguing all over again. Mel would have to go back to the Lord, and the Lord would tell him, "Look, you're not to look for a particular response from her when you apologize. I said you have to love her unconditionally!"

Before long, Mel started to do just that. He loved me

unconditionally until I broke on the inside. And when I broke, I broke deeply, because for the first time in my life I saw Christ Jesus actually manifested in a human body. Through Mel, I saw the love of Christ, which is not about who's right and who's wrong. The love of Christ is Mel saying to me, "Even though you are whiney and angry and manipulative and controlling and mean and throwing things; I am going to give you the unconditional love of Christ. I am going to believe the best about you. I am going to speak life over you and I'm just going to love you. I'm going to love you with all my life." I asked God to please make me that strong and as wonderful a person, too. When that became my desire, I wanted to be the first one to apologize and ask for forgiveness for not acting Christ-like and for allowing strife to come into our relationship. How wonderful it is when you have two people wanting to be the first to ask for forgiveness and make things right.

First Corinthians 13 is known as the love chapter of the Bible. Here's what it says:

> Though I speak with the tongues of men and of angels, but have not love, I have become sounding brass or a clanging cymbal. And though I have the gift of prophecy, and understand all mysteries and all knowledge, and though I have all faith, so that I could remove mountains, but have not love, I am nothing. And though I bestow all my goods to feed the poor, and though I give my body to be burned, but have not love, it profits me nothing.
>
> Love suffers long and is kind; love does not envy; love does not parade itself, is not puffed up; does not behave rudely, does not seek its own, is not provoked, thinks no evil; does not rejoice in iniquity, but rejoices

in the truth; bears all things, believes all things, hopes all things, endures all things.

Love never fails. But whether there are prophecies, they will fail; whether there are tongues, they will cease; whether there is knowledge, it will vanish away. For we know in part and we prophesy in part. But when that which is perfect has come, then that which is in part will be done away. When I was a child, I spoke as a child, I understood as a child, I thought as a child; but when I became a man, I put away childish things. For now we see in a mirror, dimly, but then face to face. Now I know in part, but then I shall know just as I also am known. And now abide faith, hope, love, these three; but the greatest of these is love.

Love never fails. We need to remember that. Sometimes it feels like if we walk in love in a certain situation, we're going to get stepped on, trampled on, taken advantage of, and walked over, but we need to remember what God tells us in His Word: love never fails!

But now you yourselves are to put off all these: anger, wrath, malice, blasphemy, filthy language out of your mouth. Do not lie to one another, since you have put off the old man with his deeds, and have put on the new man who is renewed in knowledge according to the image of Him who created him … Bearing with one another, and forgiving one another, if anyone has a complaint against another; even as Christ forgave you, so you also must do.

— COLOSSIANS 3:8–10, 13

It can be hard to forgive people, can't it? But just think about everything God has forgiven you for. That should make it a lot easier to forgive others. Verse 14 tells us:

"But above all these things put on love, which is the bond of perfection."

Have you ever thought or felt, "I don't have enough love for this person"? Have you ever said, "God, just give me love for this person"? I believe we all have felt like this at one time or another. What we need to do in these times is to run to God, get filled up with His love for us, and then just let Him love on us. He wants to pour out His love on us and then pour out His love through us! However, when we don't have enough love, we're like cars that need to go to the gas station for a refill: we need to go back to the Lord and get filled up with His love.

Continuing to verse 15 we read: "And let the peace of God rule in your hearts." Have you ever noticed that when you depart from love, every ounce of peace flies out the door? I love the peace of God. I'm sure you do, too. The question is: are we willing to pay the price to have that peace all the time?

> And let the peace of God rule in your hearts, to which also you were called in one body; and be thankful. Let the word of Christ dwell in you richly in all wisdom, teaching and admonishing one another in psalms and hymns and spiritual songs, singing with grace in your hearts to the Lord. And whatever you do in word or deed, do all in the name of the Lord Jesus, giving thanks to God the Father through Him.
>
> —COLOSSIANS 3:15–17

Now let's turn our attention to 1 Peter 3:8–9:

> Finally, all of you be of one mind, having compassion for one another; love as brothers, be tenderhearted, be courteous, not returning evil for evil or

reviling for reviling, but on the contrary blessing, knowing that you were called to this, that you may inherit a blessing.

There's an important message here as well. When we don't return evil and when we walk in love, we will be blessed. Sometimes things happen that require us to turn the other cheek. This may mean that we have to turn and walk away from the situation so that we don't depart from love and say the wrong thing. God promises that when we walk in love, we will receive a blessing. Therefore, you're going to inherit a blessing. Do you want to love life or do you want to hate it? If you want to love it, here's what the Word says in verse 10:

> For "He who would love life and see good days, Let him refrain his tongue from evil…"

This means that when somebody has done us wrong, we should refrain from telling anybody else about it. Even though speaking of someone in this manner may feel like the natural thing to do, the scripture above clearly shows that we should not talk to others about what the person has done.

From 1 Peter 4:8, we learn: "And above all things have fervent love for one another, for "love will cover a multitude of sins." Here it says that love *covers* a multitude of sins, not that love *exposes* a multitude of sins! Some people think that their ability to discern sin means that they're spiritually gifted. Well, that's not being spiritually gifted. A spiritually-gifted person will instead discern the call of God on people's lives, love them in spite of their sin, and encourage them to press forth to the mark of their high calling in Christ Jesus, fulfill their destiny, and someday hear the words, "Well done, good and faithful servant!" They will love people through their sin and help them fulfill the call God has on their lives. This brings us to the question: Will you love people even when they're sinning against you?

> You are of God, little children, and have overcome them, because He who is in you is greater than he who is in the world.
>
> —1 JOHN 4:4

It's so important to remember that Jesus is alive inside of you. This same Jesus was nailed to the cross. He was perfect. He never sinned. He loved people. He healed them. He was God in the flesh and came to take our place, to bridge the gap, to keep us from going to hell. While they were nailing Him to the Cross, His dying words were, "Father, forgive them, for they do not know what they do" (Luke 23:34). Even today, He still says to forgive them.

If He who says this is alive inside of us, surely we can do just that. But, we have to remember that it's impossible to forgive others in our own strength. Here's how it will always work. Remember who you are. If you've asked Jesus to come into your heart and to be your Savior and your Lord, He's in you and you're in Him. You're a Christian. A Christian is one on whom the power of God is poured all over and through. Philippians 4:13 says:

> I can do all things through Christ [through the anointed One and His anointing] who strengthens me.

Through Christ, it is possible for you to forgive others. God would never ask you to do something you couldn't do.

He would never tell you to do something that's going to hurt you. He's telling you to forgive so that you don't stay in your anorexic or bulimic behavior, so you won't be taken out with cancer, so that your back will stop hurting, so that the pain in your body will go away. He wants the pain out of your heart and He wants it out of your body. God wants you to prosper and be in health, even as your soul prospers. (See 3 John 2.)

So forgive others. You can do it. Receive His forgiveness and allow yourself to forgive yourself as well. If God has forgiven you, who are you not to do the same? Don't allow the enemy's lies to keep you from the fullness of your relationship with the Lord and from the fullness of the life and work He has planned just for you. Romans 8:1–2 says:

> There is therefore now no condemnation to those who are in Christ Jesus, who do not walk according to the flesh, but according to the Spirit. For the law of the Spirit of life in Christ Jesus has made me free from the law of sin and death.

Understand and receive this Word from the Lord as true and final in your life!

At this juncture, I want to draw your heart and attention back again to how very much your heavenly Father loves you. He adores you. Read and meditate on this beautiful letter He has written to you. Once you receive His Word, receive this Word as true, you will never be the same...and it really will be possible for you to live as the vessel of His love that you were created to be!

My Child,

> ♥ You may not know Me, but I know everything about you (Ps. 139:1).

🌹 Even the very hairs on your head are numbered (Matt. 10:30).

🌹 For you were made in My image (Gen. 1:27).

🌹 I knew you even before you were conceived (Jer. 1:5).

🌹 I chose you when I planned creation (Eph. 1:11).

🌹 And I knit you together in your mother's womb (Ps. 139:13).

🌹 You are not a mistake, for all your days are written in My book (Ps. 139:16).

🌹 I determined when you would be born and where you would live (Acts 17:26).

🌹 I love you with an everlasting love (Jer. 31:3).

🌹 I have been misrepresented by those who don't know Me (John 8:41–44).

🌹 I am not distant and angry but am the complete expression of love (1 John 4:16).

🌹 It is My desire to lavish My love on you (1 John 3:1).

🌹 For every good gift that you receive comes from My hand (James 1:17).

🌹 I offer you more than your earthly father ever could… (Matt. 7:11).

🌹 …because I am the perfect Father… (Matt. 5:48).

❤ ...and I am the provider who meets all your needs (Matt. 6:11–33).

❤ My plan for your future has always been filled with hope (Jer. 29:11).

❤ My thoughts toward you are as countless as the sand on the seashore... (Ps. 139:17–18).

❤ ...and I "rejoice over you with singing" (Zeph. 3:17).

❤ I will never stop doing good to you... (Jer. 32:40).

❤ ...for you are My treasured possession (Exod. 19:5).

❤ Delight in Me and I will give you the desires of your heart... (Ps. 37:4).

❤ ...for it is I who gave you those desires (Phil. 2:13).

❤ I am able to do more for you than you could possibly imagine... (Eph. 3:20–21).

❤ ...for I am your greatest encourager (2 Thess. 2:16–17).

❤ I am also the Father who comforts you in all your troubles (2 Cor. 1:3–4).

❤ When you are brokenhearted, I am close to you (Ps. 34:18).

❤ As a shepherd carries a lamb, I have carried you close to my heart (Isa. 40:11).

🌱 One day I will wipe every tear from your eyes
(Rev. 21:3–4).

🌱 Because I love you even as I love My son, Jesus
(John 17:23).

🌱 For in Jesus, My love for you is revealed
(John 17:23).

🌱 He is the exact representation of My being
(Heb. 1:3).

🌱 He came to demonstrate that I am for you, not
against you… (Rom. 8:31).

🌱 …and to tell you that I am not counting your sins
(2 Cor. 5:18–19).

🌱 Jesus died so that you could be reconciled
(2 Cor. 5:18–19).

🌱 His death was My ultimate expression of love for
you (1 John 4:10).

🌱 I gave up everything that I loved to gain your love
(Rom. 8:32).

🌱 If you receive the gift of My Son, you receive Me
(1 John 2:23).

🌱 And nothing will ever separate you from My love
again (Rom. 8:38–39).

🌱 Come home and I'll throw the biggest party
heaven has ever seen (Luke 15:7).

❦ I have always been Father, and will always be
Father (Eph. 3:14–15).

❦ My question is: will you be my child?
(John 1:12–13).

—Your Loving Heavenly Father[2]

Now, pray this simple prayer with me.

*Father God, I love You. I thank You for sending Jesus.
Jesus, thank You for dying on the cross and being raised
from the dead. Thank You for coming into my heart, for
being my Lord, my Savior, my healer, my best friend.
Forgive me for every sin that I've committed. I forgive
everyone who's hurt me. Thank You for helping me to
let the hurt go. I let it go now, in Jesus' name! Forgive
me, Father, for having any and all unforgivingness in
my heart. Heal my heart. Fill me with your Holy Spirit,
with every gift You have for me. I yield to You, Holy
Spirit. Have your way in me. Change my heart and help
me to be the peaceful, strong, healthy vessel of your love
that You created me to be. In Jesus' name, amen.*

6

Nutrition and Exercise

HEALTHY EATING CAN be delicious and exercising can be fun. Let's just decide that it's going to be! Just as God can renew your mind through His Word, your taste buds can be renewed. You can actually enjoy exercise and have a spiritual experience while working out. I believe that God will do a "new thing" in your life and you'll enjoy eating fruits, vegetables, lean proteins, and grains. You'll love drinking lots of water and you'll look forward to exercising if you allow Him to renew your mind and thought processes in this area of your life. You do not have to stay in your present condition.

First, let's see what the Bible says about exercise: "For bodily exercise profits a little" (1 Tim. 4:8). Now I want to point out that this verse doesn't say bodily exercise profits *nothing*. If it did, then I wouldn't be teaching anything about it. It says it profits a *little*. I believe it says "little" because heaven is long and earth is short. Most of us will live seventy to eighty years here on earth. That is a little bit of time compared to heaven where we will live for eternity in our glorified bodies. And when we go to heaven, we're not taking this body with us. We'll be taking our spirit man with us, so exercising our spirit man is what is most important.

Nonetheless, while we're alive here on earth, we still need to take care of our physical bodies and do all we can to glorify God in every part of our lives. None of us want to be sick or have pain in our body. Who doesn't love to feel good and be healthy? Here's how the Amplified version phrases 1 Timothy 4:8:

> For physical training is of some value (useful for a little), but godliness (spiritual training) is useful and of value in everything and in every way, for it holds promise for the present life and also for the life which is to come.

There's balance in all of this. Beginning with exercise, we understand that we should engage in some kind of physical activity on a regular basis. The challenge here is usually consistency. But how do you stay consistent?

One of the ways you can do this is to make your exercising a spiritual experience. For this very reason, I produced an exercise video and DVD called, *Spirit, Soul & Body Workout*.[1] I found that when I went to the gym to work out, I didn't like some of the lyrics in the music we were exercising to, such as, "Slam your head into the wall." So, I created a workout video that has anointed music, which ministers to you while you exercise. Of course, you can also put on your favorite CD and stretch, dance, or exercise to that. Or you can walk and pray and talk to God all at the same time.

One of my favorite ways to exercise is to swim in the pool, kicking on my kickboard and praying in the Spirit. That way I get my little bit of profit from bodily exercise, but I am also getting the greater profit of exercising my spirit man. First Corinthians 14:4 says, "He who speaks in a [strange] tongue edifies and improves himself" (AMP). I suggest that you get your body toned and in shape, and edify your complete person—body, soul, and spirit all at the same time—by exercising as you pray in the Spirit.

Another great activity is to hike or walk with a friend so you can have good fellowship for your mind and spirit while exercising your body. Instead of setting a time to get together and enjoy a meal, you could plan to exercise together. Have some fun and build relationships while you're at it!

If you're happy with the way you look and feel and want to stay that way, my recommendation is that you exercise three times a week with a program you enjoy. Some people love the water and some like to walk. Some people like to exercise to a video, which is particularly helpful because you can exercise according your own schedule and build up your stamina at your own pace.

If you want to improve or change the way you look, you need to work out more often, perhaps four to six times per week. If you work out two times a week or less, sooner or later, you will become out of shape. Sorry, there's just no way around that. Even the Apostle Paul exercised and disciplined his body. He learned to keep it under control. His words are recorded for us in Acts:

> Therefore I always exercise and discipline myself [mortifying my body, deadening my carnal affections, bodily appetites, and worldly desires, endeavoring in all respects] to have a clear (unshaken, blameless) conscience, void of offense toward God and toward men.
>
> —ACTS 24:16, AMP

As it says in 1 Corinthians 6:19-20, our bodies are supposed to glorify the Lord:

> Or do you not know that your body is the temple of the Holy Spirit who is in you, whom you have from God, and you are not your own? For you were bought at a price; therefore glorify God in your body and in your spirit, which are God's.

This same portion of Scripture is particularly impacting when we read the translation in *The Message*:

> You know the old saying, "First you eat to live, and then you live to eat"? Well, it may be true that the body is only a temporary thing, but that's no excuse for stuffing your body with food, or indulging it with sex. Since the Master honors you with a body, honor Him with your body!
>
> God honored the Master's body by raising it from the grave. He'll treat yours with the same resurrection power. Until that time, remember that your bodies are created with the same dignity as the Master's body. You wouldn't take the Master's body off to a whorehouse, would you? I should hope not....
>
> Or didn't you realize that your body is a sacred place, the place of the Holy Spirit? Don't you see that you can't live however you please, squandering what God paid such a high price for? The physical part of you is not some piece of property belonging to the spiritual part of you. God owns the whole works. So let people see God in and through your body.
> —1 CORINTHIANS 6:13–15, 19–20

FOOD AND NUTRITION

The Bible has a lot more to say about food and nutrition than it does about bodily exercise. Much of my testimony and the tremendous victory in breaking free of anorexia and bulimia had to do with learning how to eat the right foods.

In some ways, getting free of an eating disorder is more difficult than getting free of drugs, alcohol, or other addictions. This is because, unlike drugs and alcohol, you cannot say, "I am never going to eat again."

Follow the Holy Spirit's lead

A major key to someone having victory in the area of eating disorders is to learn how to be led by the Holy Spirit in what you eat. You see, it's not a diet and it's not a routine. Instead, it's about what you do every time you step foot into a restaurant, or when you're cooking at home, or begin to fill your cart at the grocery store. You need to be led by the Holy Spirit in every decision you make about eating. In fact, you need to be led by the Holy Spirit whenever you deal with food.

I want to make something very clear. Jesus setting you free of something does not mean that you're always going to have to battle it, or that it will always be an area of weakness for you. It will only be a weakness and you'll only have to battle it if you don't know and incorporate the Word of God into your life regarding that area.

This reminds me of a story I once read that ministered to me. Kenneth Copeland responded to the following comment in an unexpected way: "Brother Copeland, I heard you mention on one of your broadcasts that some years ago God delivered you from a weight problem that had plagued you all your life."

His response was:

First of all let me make a very important correction. God didn't deliver me from a weight problem. He delivered me from a food problem. God showed me that I wanted to lose weight, but I didn't want to permanently change my eating habits. I was like an alcoholic who wants to be able to drink constantly and not be affected by it. I wanted to eat nine times a day and still weigh 165 pounds. I was a glutton who wanted to continue in my gluttony and somehow escape the consequences. God couldn't be a partner to that. In His Word, He put gluttony in the same category with drunkenness. It's a sin. And in my prayers I'd actually been asking God to help me get away with this sin. No wonder those prayers had gone unanswered.

So I changed my prayers. First I repented of the sin of gluttony. It hurts to admit something like that. But instead of asking God for deliverance from my weight problem, I asked Him for deliverance from my food problem. God told me, *I'm not going to deliver you from food all together.* He said, *just from certain kinds of food.* The Lord assured me that He was fully capable of changing my appetite so that I would actually enjoy foods that were good for me. And sure enough, He did. Food is no longer a problem for me! The same thing can happen to you if you go to the Lord and you ask for deliverance, not just from the weight problem you're suffering from but from the food problem that very well may be behind it. Spend time in the Word. Spend time in prayer. Let Him show you what the source of trouble is. Don't just ask Him to change your looks. Ask Him to change your life. I know from experience, He'll do it."[2]

It's really not that hard

With God's help, eating foods that are good for you can be easy. Healthy eating is choosing the food that God created. Before you put something in your mouth to eat, ask yourself, *Did God make this food?* His food is always the best for us. Eating a potato raw, in its purest form, is the healthiest for you. Baking it—that's second-best. Turn it into a French fry, and we've added the grease that is not good for you. From there, if we take almost everything out, we have the potato chip! This is what man does to God's food. We turn something that is good for us into something that is bad for us.

Have you ever seen people who seem to be able to eat anything and everything and still stay thin? On the other hand, other people hardly eat a thing and still put on weight. A lot of that has to do with metabolism. Here are three easy ways to speed up your metabolism:

1. Exercise, as we discussed earlier in this chapter.
2. Speak the Word of God over yourself.

In Matthew 15:11 it says, "Not what goes into the mouth defiles a man; but what comes out of the mouth, this defiles a man." I can't overemphasize how important it is to speak the Word of God over yourself. Even worse for you than eating processed food is having words come out of your mouth that are ungodly, negative words over your life and the lives of others.

3. Eat small portions of food four to six times a day.

Choose healthy foods such as fresh fruits, raw vegetables, lean proteins, and whole grains. Several small portions of healthy natural foods throughout the day will keep the fire of your metabolism revved up and help you burn calories.

I also want to address fasting. I believe in fasting because God tells us to fast. But here's the key, did God call you into a fast for a particular spiritual reason or are you fasting to lose weight? When God calls you into a fast, I believe God supernaturally protects your metabolism. He would never ask you to do anything that would bring harm to your body. However, if you're fasting to lose weight, you could be doing more harm than good. Trying to lose weight by not eating at all actually slows down your metabolism. In turn, it becomes easier to put on weight and makes it harder to lose weight in the long run.

But what happens if you're following God's way of eating and exercising, and you blow it? What do you do? You get back up and try again. Don't quit because you may have blown it. You'll win this battle if you don't give up. When you slip or stumble in your new plan, you may be inclined to beat yourself up with guilt or self-condemnation. This in itself is a "weight" in the spirit realm, which will then manifest itself in the natural realm. Knowing this, simply pick yourself up and say, "I *am* going to win this battle because I'm God's child and destined for victory. I will be led by the Spirit, and not the flesh."

Romans 8:1–4 declares our freedom from guilt and condemnation:

> THEREFORE, [there is] now no condemnation (no adjudging guilty of wrong) for those who are in Christ Jesus, who live [and] walk not after the dictates of the flesh, but after the dictates of the Spirit. For the law of the Spirit of life [which is] in Christ Jesus [the law of our new being] has freed me from the law of sin

and death. For God has done what the Law could not do, [its power] being weakened by the flesh [the entire nature of man without the Holy Spirit]. Sending His own Son in the guise of sinful flesh and as an offering for sin, [God] condemned sin in the flesh [subdued, overcame, deprived it of its power over all who accept that sacrifice], So that the righteous and just requirement of the Law might be fully met in us who live and move not in the ways of the flesh but in the ways of the Spirit [our lives governed not by the standards and according to the dictates of the flesh, but controlled by the Holy Spirit].

—AMP

This portion of Scripture may be applied to any battle between the flesh and the spirit with which you are struggling. Everyone can relate to the struggle with food, but the same principles for victory may be applied to other struggles.

For those who are according to the flesh and are controlled by its unholy desires set their minds on and pursue those things which gratify the flesh, but those who are according to the Spirit and are controlled by the desires of the Spirit set their minds on and seek those things which gratify the [Holy] Spirit.

—ROMANS 8:5, AMP

So much of who we are is determined by where our minds are focused. Whatever your area of weakness, we can liken it to, say, chocolate cake. If your weakness is chocolate cake, what do you think will happen if one day you go into a bakery and stare at a double-layer fudge cake? That's right; you'll buy it and eat it if you don't stop focusing on that cake! Don't look at it; turn away from it.

A war is going on and you are in the middle of it! It is a daily battle between walking in the Spirit and walking in the flesh. For some who have a problem with pornography, it may be the choice between getting on the Internet late at night or only when the family is awake and nearby. Or it may be the choice to either eat the chocolate cake that will throw your energy level off and make you fat or to eat good food that will nourish and fuel your body for the purpose of fulfilling your divine destiny. Whatever the struggle, the daily battle is as much over your focus as it is over the choice itself. If you have been focusing on God and accomplishing the strategies given in this book, you will be partaking of what is healthy for you, blesses others, and glorifies God. The choice begins and ends with following God's battle plan.

Continuing in the teaching on the war between the spirit and the flesh, let's look at the following passage:

> [That is] because the mind of the flesh [with its carnal thoughts and purposes] is hostile to God, for it does not submit itself to God's Law; indeed it cannot. So then those who are living the life of the flesh [catering to the appetites and impulses of their carnal nature] cannot please or satisfy God, or be acceptable to Him. But you are not living the life of the flesh, you are living the life of the Spirit, if the [Holy] Spirit of God [really] dwells within you [directs and controls you]. But if anyone does not possess the [Holy] Spirit of Christ, he is none of His [he does not belong to Christ, is not truly a child of God]. But if Christ lives in you, [then although] your [natural] body is dead by reason of sin and guilt, the spirit is alive because of [the] righteousness [that He imputes

to you]. And if the Spirit of Him Who raised up Jesus from the dead dwells in you, [then] He Who raised up Christ Jesus from the dead will also restore to life your mortal (short-lived, perishable) bodies through His Spirit Who dwells in you.

—ROMANS 8:7–11, AMP

Can you see how important it is to be led by the Holy Spirit, even in the area of eating? Can food kill you? Yes, if you eat unhealthy foods often enough and long enough, you just may miss out on finishing the years of productivity that the Lord has for you.

So then, brethren, we are debtors, but not to the flesh [we are not obligated to our carnal nature], to live [a life ruled by the standards set up by the dictates] of the flesh. For if you live according to [the dictates of] the flesh, you will surely die. But if through the power of the [Holy] Spirit you are [habitually] putting to death (making extinct, deadening) the [evil] deeds prompted by the body, you shall [really and genuinely] live forever. For all who are led by the Spirit of God are sons of God.

—ROMANS 8:12–14, AMP

Our mind is where the battle between what God wants us to do and what the devil wants us to do is waged!

We may be hit with thoughts like: "I know I should eat fruits, vegetables, and whole grains, but I saw a thin person eat a big piece of birthday cake at a party. If she can eat it, surely I should be able to. In fact, why can't I just eat the whole cake? And why can't I eat whatever I want, whenever I want? Why do I have to live this way and deprive myself? This is tough! It's not fair! Why can't I just eat what I want to?"

When this happens, remember to overcome those harmful, negative thoughts by casting them down and replacing them with positive ones.

> Casting down arguments and every high thing that exalts itself against the knowledge of God, bringing every thought into captivity to the obedience of Christ.
>
> —2 CORINTHIANS 10:5

After casting those negative and unproductive thoughts down, choose what you will now think on and say words like, "You know what, it doesn't matter what anyone else is eating, I'm not responsible for them. I'm responsible for myself, and I'm going to make good choices for my body. I will eat healthy foods!" Ephesians 4:23 says, "And be renewed in the spirit of your mind." That means you have to change the way you think.

Did you know that your taste buds can be renewed just like your mind can be renewed? When you're fasting or go a long period of time without eating for some other reason, whatever you put into your body first is what you will end up craving later. When you're extremely hungry, any food tastes good. Food can actually taste ten times better than it would normally taste if you weren't hungry. That's why it's so important to be careful about what you choose to eat when you are extremely hungry.

Many people will not eat breakfast or lunch, but then at around mid-afternoon will drive through a fast-food line to buy something unhealthy. From then on, whenever they're really hungry, they will crave that very thing because they will consciously or subconsciously remember how good it tasted. If they had filled their hunger with a nice healthy salad, they would crave salad the next time they are very hungry.

I like what my husband, Mel, says, "Feed the good dog; starve the bad dog!" What you choose to eat when you're hungry is what you'll crave. Let's turn our attention now to Romans 12:1–2:

> I beseech you therefore, brethren, by the mercies of God, that you present your bodies a living sacrifice, holy, acceptable to God, which is your reasonable service. And do not be conformed to this world, but be transformed by the renewing of your mind, that you may prove what is that good and acceptable and perfect will of God.

I believe this scripture can set you free from any eating disorder, any bondage of alcohol, any addiction to drugs, or any past hurt that still plagues you and keeps you from going forward to fulfill your divine destiny. It's key. *"Be transformed by the renewing of your mind!"*(Rom. 12:2).

We're all in the process of being changed. As we change, let's also grow up in our knowledge of God and walk with Him in every area of our lives, even in the area of what we eat and how we exercise our bodies. It's such a blessing that as His children we can do that. He tells us that He's begun a good work in each of us, and that He's faithful to complete that work until He returns. This means that daily we're being transformed into the image of Christ if we're willing to change and grow. And how do we change and grow? By renewing our minds through reading the Word of God and deciding, "That's the truth, and anything less than that is not!" It's a choice that you and I have to make.

For most of us, how we think reflects what our parents believed and focused on. But we still have our own choices to make. The good news is that in Christ we can be transformed by the renewing of our minds as we pursue Him and obey what He says in His Word.

Consider applying Philippians 4:8 to your life daily:

> … Whatever things are true, whatever things are noble, whatever things are just, whatever things are pure, whatever things are lovely, whatever things are of good report, if there is any virtue and if there is anything praiseworthy—meditate on these things.

I challenge you to go for one week and just think on the good things in your life. Think about and focus on what is good for you to eat and see yourself enjoying taking care of your body with regular exercise. For seven days, speak only those things that are true, just, lovely, and a good report about yourself and others. That's really how we're to talk anyway. Are you up to that challenge? I encourage you to give it a try. With God's help, learn to think on and speak only good things about others and about yourself.

As we conclude this book, I pray 1 Thessalonians 5:23 for you:

> And may the God of peace Himself sanctify you through and through [separate you from profane things, make you pure and wholly consecrated to God]; and may your spirit and soul and body be preserved sound and complete [and found] blameless at the coming of our Lord Jesus Christ (the Messiah).
>
> —AMP

I invite you to pray this prayer with me:

> *Father God, I thank You so much for Your presence in my life and for what You are about to do even now. I*

thank You that every stronghold, every addiction, every generational curse is broken off me, in the name of Jesus. Thank You for healing my heart and restoring my soul in any area where that is needed. I receive Your joy, Your strength, Your life, and Your peace. I thank You, Lord that I love to eat healthy foods. I love to exercise. Thank You that my weight is in a normal, healthy range, which is an honor to You and which is helpful in my living a long and prosperous life. Thank You for the blood of Jesus, which bought my freedom and healing. Thank You, Holy Spirit. Have Your way in my heart and life. In Jesus' name, amen.

To Contact the Author

In conclusion, it is my heart's desire that you have been encouraged and gained some truth to set you free on your life's journey. Please write me and let me know the good news that is taking place in your life. I would love to hear from you. If you need prayer, please do not hesitate to contact me so I can stand in agreement with you. God bless you abundantly on your road to victory! You will win if you don't quit!

Please write to:

Desiree Ayres
In His Presence Church
21300 Califa Street
Woodland Hills, CA 91357

E-mail: Godhunger@ihpchurch.org

The *Spirit, Soul, and Body Exercise Video* is a sixty-minute low-impact workout taught by Desiree Ayres. The original, anointed music will encourage you to work out, look good, and radiate! The exercise video and other teaching material are available through our online bookstore at www.ihpchurch.org.

Appendix

GOD HUNGER SCRIPTURES

I WOULD LIKE TO leave with you the scriptures that I stood on for my complete healing. I found these scriptures when I read the Book of Matthew through Revelation asking God to speak to me about my food disorder.

> But He replied, It has been written, Man shall not live and be upheld and sustained by bread alone, but by every word that comes forth from the mouth of God.
> —MATTHEW 4:4, AMP

> Therefore I tell you, stop being perpetually uneasy (anxious and worried) about your life, what you shall eat or what you shall drink; or about your body, what you shall put on. Is not life greater [in quality] than food, and the body [far above and more excellent] than clothing?
> —MATTHEW 6:25, AMP

> Look at the birds of the air; they neither sow nor reap nor gather into barns, and yet your heavenly Father

keeps feeding them. Are you not worth much more than they?

—MATTHEW 6:26, AMP

But seek (aim at and strive after) first of all His kingdom and His righteousness (His way of doing and being right), and then all these things taken together will be given you besides. So do not worry or be anxious about tomorrow, for tomorrow will have worries and anxieties of its own. Sufficient for each day is its own trouble.

—MATTHEW 6:33–34, AMP

It is not what goes into the mouth of a man that makes him unclean and defiled, but what comes out of the mouth; this makes a man unclean and defiles [him].

—MATTHEW 15:11, AMP

Keep awake and watch and pray [constantly], that you may not enter into temptation; the spirit indeed is willing, but the flesh is weak.

—MARK 14:38, AMP

There is not [even] one thing outside a man which by going into him can pollute and defile him, but the things which come out of a man are what defile him and make him unhallowed and unclean.

—MARK 7:15, AMP

Man shall not live and be sustained by (on) bread alone but by every word and expression of God.

—LUKE 4:4, AMP

Jesus answered her, All who drink of this water will be thirsty again. But whoever takes a drink of the water that I will give him shall never, no never, be thirsty any more. But the water that I will give him shall become

a spring of water welling up (flowing, bubbling) [con-
tinually] within him unto (into, for) eternal life.

—JOHN 4:13–14, AMP

Stop toiling and doing and producing for the food that
perishes and decomposes [in the using]; but strive
and work and produce rather for the lasting food
which endures [continually] unto life eternal; the Son
of Man will give (furnish) you that, for God the Father
has authorized and certified Him and put His seal of
endorsement upon Him.

—JOHN 6:27, AMP

For the Bread of God is He Who comes down out of
heaven and gives life to the world.

—JOHN 6:33, AMP

Jesus replied, I am the Bread of Life. He who comes to
Me will never be hungry and he who believes in and
cleaves to and trusts in and relies on Me will never
thirst anymore (at any time).

—JOHN 6:35, AMP

And if the Spirit of Him Who raised up Jesus from
the dead dwell in you [then] He Who raised up Christ
Jesus from the dead will also restore to life your mortal (short-lived, perishable) bodies through His Spirit
Who dwells in you.

—ROMANS 8:11, AMP

Clothe yourself with the Lord Jesus Christ (the Mes-
siah), and make no provision for [indulging] the flesh
[put a stop to thinking about the evil cravings of your
physical nature] to [gratify its] desires (lusts).

—ROMANS 13:14, AMP

But I say, walk and live [habitually] in the [Holy] Spirit [responsive to and controlled and guided by the Spirit]; then you will certainly not gratify the cravings and desires of the flesh (of human nature without God).

—GALATIANS 5:16, AMP

For God did not give us a spirit of timidity (of cowardice, of craven and cringing and fawning fear), but [He has given us a spirit] of power and of love and of calm and well-balanced mind and discipline and self-control.

—2 TIMOTHY 1:7, AMP

For we all often stumble and fall and offend in many things. And if anyone does not offend in speech [never says the wrong things], he is a fully developed character and a perfect man, able to control his whole body and to curb his entire nature.

—JAMES 3:2, AMP

So that he can no longer spend the rest of his natural life living by [his] human appetites and desires, but [he lives] for what God wills.

—1 PETER 4:2, AMP

Little children keep yourselves from idols (false gods)—[from anything and everything that would occupy the place in your heart due to God, from any sort of substitute for Him that would take first place in your life].

—1 JOHN 5:21, AMP

Notes

Preface

1. Thomas Costain, *The Three Edwards* (New York: Buccaneer Books, 1994).

Introduction

1. For more information see http://www.eatingdisorderinfo.org/18.html.
2. Ibid.
3. Ibid.
4. Ibid.
5. Ibid.
6. Ibid.
7. Ibid.
8. Ibid.
9. For more information see http://www.nationaleatingdisorders.org/ p.asp?WebPage_ID=286&Profile_ID=41138

10. For more information see http://www.eatingdisorderinfo. org/18.html.

11. For more information see http://win.niddk.nih.gov/ statistics/index.htm.

12. For more information see http://www.usatoday.com/ news/health/2003-05-13-obesity-usat_x.htm.

13. See Deut. 3:22, 20:4; 3 John 11; 1 Cor. 15:57; 2 Cor. 3:17 (RSV); Deut. 30:9, Ps. 37:4; Rom. 16:27; Eph. 1:18; Matt. 6:33; Phil. 4:15.

2
Who Told You, You Are Fat?

1. Marianne Williamson, *A Return to Love* (New York: Harper Paperbacks, 1996).

4
Two Tools for Achieving Your Desired Weight

1. Pastor Casey Treat, Vision International Leadership Conference, March 2001.

2. Quote available at http://www.navpress.com/Magazines/ Pray!/PrinterFriendlyArticle.asp?ID=005.19. Accessed 9/27/05.

3. Kenneth Copeland, *Prayer: Your Foundation for Success* (Forth Worth, TX: Kenneth Copeland Publications, 1999).

4. Quote available at http://psalm121.ca/quotes/dcqwesley. html. Accessed 9/27/05.

5. David Watson, *Called & Committed*, (Wheaton, IL: Harold Shaw Publishers, 1982), 83.

5
PUT OFF EXTRA WEIGHTS

1. Desiree Ayres, *Beyond the Flame.* Release date 2007.
2. *Father's Love Letter*, Barry Adams. Used by permission. Father's Heart Communications, copyright © 1999–2004. www.FathersLoveLetter.com.

6
NUTRITION AND EXERCISE

1. To order visit www. ihpchurch.org.
2. "Questions and Answers," *Believers' Voice of Victory,* October/November 1988, 7.